Cambridge Elements

Elements in Ancient Philosophy
edited by
James Warren
University of Cambridge

PLATO'S UNWRITTEN DOCTRINES

Carl Séan O'Brien
Irish Dominican House of Studies

Shaftesbury Road, Cambridge CB2 8EA, United Kingdom

One Liberty Plaza, 20th Floor, New York, NY 10006, USA

477 Williamstown Road, Port Melbourne, VIC 3207, Australia

314–321, 3rd Floor, Plot 3, Splendor Forum, Jasola District Centre, New Delhi – 110025, India

103 Penang Road, #05–06/07, Visioncrest Commercial, Singapore 238467

Cambridge University Press is part of Cambridge University Press & Assessment, a department of the University of Cambridge.

We share the University's mission to contribute to society through the pursuit of education, learning and research at the highest international levels of excellence.

www.cambridge.org
Information on this title: www.cambridge.org/9781009506175
DOI: 10.1017/9781009506212

© Carl Séan O'Brien 2025

This publication is in copyright. Subject to statutory exception and to the provisions of relevant collective licensing agreements, no reproduction of any part may take place without the written permission of Cambridge University Press & Assessment.

When citing this work, please include a reference to the DOI 10.1017/9781009506212

First published 2025

A catalogue record for this publication is available from the British Library

ISBN 978-1-009-50617-5 Hardback
ISBN 978-1-009-50620-5 Paperback
ISSN 2631-4118 (online)
ISSN 2631-410X (print)

Cambridge University Press & Assessment has no responsibility for the persistence or accuracy of URLs for external or third-party internet websites referred to in this publication and does not guarantee that any content on such websites is, or will remain, accurate or appropriate.

For EU product safety concerns, contact us at Calle de José Abascal, 56, 1°, 28003 Madrid, Spain, or email eugpsr@cambridge.org

Plato's Unwritten Doctrines

Elements in Ancient Philosophy

DOI: 10.1017/9781009506212
First published online: September 2025

Carl Séan O'Brien
Irish Dominican House of Studies

Author for correspondence: Carl Séan O'Brien, obriencs@tcd.ie

Abstract: This Element examines the arguments advanced by the Tübingen–Milan School in support of the claim that Plato had Unwritten Doctrines (*agrapha dogmata*), revealed in Aristotle and other testimonia and indicated – but not explicitly treated – in some of his dialogues. The Unwritten Doctrines are primarily concerned with Plato's Theory of Principles (the One and the Indefinite Dyad) which accounts for unity and multiplicity respectively. This Element considers two opposing approaches to reading Plato: that of *sola scriptura* (through the writings alone) or via the tradition. While it may appear counter-intuitive to privilege other sources over Plato's own works, his criticism of writing in the *Phaedrus* and the 'deliberate gaps', where he teases the reader with the possibility of a fuller response than that provided on the current occasion, firmly indicate the existence of doctrines not committed to his dialogues.

Keywords: Plato, Principles, Tübingen School, Schleiermacher, One, Indefinite Dyad, History of Platonism

© Carl Séan O'Brien 2025

ISBNs: 9781009506175 (HB), 9781009506205 (PB), 9781009506212 (OC)
ISSNs: 2631-4118 (online), 2631-410X (print)

Contents

1 What Are the Unwritten Doctrines?   1

2 Plato's Criticism of Writing   11

3 Plato's Theory of Principles and the Testimonia   26

4 Consequences of the Tübingen School Approach for Later Platonism   39

5 Critics of the Unwritten Doctrines   49

6 Conclusion   58

   List of Abbreviations   64

   References   65

1 What Are the Unwritten Doctrines?

1.1 Introduction

To assert that a philosopher and a literary artist like Plato, who left such a significant and extensive corpus of works behind, had unwritten doctrines – *agrapha dogmata* – (i.e. doctrines not discussed at length in his corpus) might initially seem like a strange claim. Even if one accepts that Plato did present an oral teaching strictly within the confines of the Academy, there is a further methodological problem: at this distance in time from Plato, how could one convincingly advance a case for such doctrines or reconstruct his oral teachings? Surely it would be self-contradictory to extract evidence for unwritten doctrines by examining Plato's writings.

This Element examines the interpretation of Plato presented by the Tübingen School, which, while largely 'unfashionable' in Anglo-American scholarship, has proven influential outside the university town from which it derives its name.[1] Whether or not we choose to accept the conclusions drawn by the Tübingen School, its approach brings into sharp focus a number of key issues. Are Plato's own dialogues exempt from his criticism of writing? What is Plato's characteristic doctrine? How do we explain those passages in the dialogues where Plato's Socrates hints that there is something more that he could reveal, but yet he explicitly chooses not to? How do we explain the attempts to systematise Plato among his original heirs, the Old Academy, which at first glance seem to display only a loose connection with the philosophy expounded in the dialogues? What does it mean to study Plato? Do we focus solely on the dialogues themselves or should we be open to considering the tradition surrounding him (as revealed in various testimonia)? How useful are these testimonia as a source for the views of Plato and his disciples? How were the dialogues originally used? Were they intended for a wider circulation among the general public or were they only employed for teaching within the confines of the Academy among Plato's inner circle? If they were widely published, then how do they relate to philosophical study within the Academy? The Tübingen School provides a coherent overarching solution to all of these questions, and by reflecting on these issues we can come to a deeper understanding of Plato.

1.2 What Are the Unwritten Doctrines?

Aristotle alerts us to Plato's ἄγραφα δόγματα ('unwritten doctrines', by which he means doctrines not treated explicitly in the dialogues) at *Physics* 209b11–209b16:

---

[1] Hösle 2019: 328 points out that this honour highlights the achievement of a small group of scholars.

> On account of this Plato says in the *Timaeus* that matter and space are the same. For the participant and space are one and the same. It is certainly true that what he says there about the participant is different from what he says in what is called the 'Unwritten Doctrines'. Nevertheless, he declared place and space to be the same. For while everyone claims that place is something, only Plato attempted to say what it is.[2]

This passage is of particular interest since Aristotle explicitly claims an oral doctrine for Plato which differs from his views in the *Timaeus* (a late dialogue and therefore reflective of Plato's mature opinions).[3] How should we interpret the dialogues (Plato's own published work), then, in light of such testimonia (claims made by others on his behalf)?[4] This raises the obvious question of how reliable a witness Aristotle is. Given the length of time he spent at the Academy, however, it seems that he would be well placed to know the teachings of the master (see Section 5.2).

What are these Unwritten Doctrines? Although not discussed explicitly in the dialogues, these doctrines are not actively concealed.[5] The Unwritten Doctrines, according to this evidence, primarily consisted of a Theory of Principles as well as views on the Form-Numbers and the essence of the soul. There are two principles: the One, τὸ ἕν – the First Principle – and the Indefinite Dyad, ἀόριστος δυάς – or the Great-and-Small, μέγα καὶ μικρόν.[6] The One is the principle of unity, while the Indefinite Dyad accounts for multiplicity (see Section 3). These principles are the causes of everything else and serve to explain how the multiplicity of the cosmos can be derived from unity. (It is essential that the ontologically prior principle is simple and therefore exhibits unity or 'oneness' since if it were a composite, it could always be split into its component parts, which would be prior to it.) Plato's principles reflect his own intellectual inheritance: the One of the Eleatics and the Many of the Ionians.[7]

This Theory of Principles may be, in fact, the most characteristic and central Platonic teaching, not the Theory of Forms. Famously, Plato himself raises doubts about the Theory of Forms in the *Parmenides*, but yet it is a prerequisite for understanding the *Timaeus*, generally thought to be a later dialogue. It is therefore difficult to maintain that Plato himself abandoned the Theory of Forms. Such claims regarding Plato's core doctrines are significant since they have implications

---

[2] Unless otherwise noted, translations are my own.
[3] This dating was challenged by Owen 1953, who claimed it as a 'middle' dialogue.
[4] Obviously, there is a distinction between what 'publication' in antiquity involved compared to today.
[5] Cf. Broadie 2021: 106 for a treatment by a non-Tübingen scholar.
[6] Aristotle identifies the Great and Small with the Dyad at *Met.* 1088a15 and with matter at *Physics* 187a15–187a20.
[7] Hösle 2019: 340. Cf. the somewhat different emphasis at Krämer 1990: 78.

for whether our view of his work is unitarian (displaying a systematic unity across the dialogues, the dominant view in antiquity) or developmentalist (revealing a shift in Plato's philosophical position over time, popular since the nineteenth century following Friedrich Schleiermacher (1768–1834)).

The Theory of Principles raises a string of further questions. How does Plato derive all other entities from these two principles, and how do these principles relate to each other? If Plato posits two principles, is he a dualist? Alternatively, if one principle outranks the other, is he a monist (see Section 3)? For the moment, we are concerned with just one central issue: how do the Unwritten Doctrines relate to the philosophy of Plato which we can derive from the dialogues? One approach is to accept at least some of Aristotle's testimony, but to marginalise the principles by confining them to the final years of Plato's life.[8] This allows everyone to save face: Aristotle is treated as credible and, due to the claim that Plato never managed to reflect the new insights offered by his Theory of Principles in any dialogue, we can continue to read his corpus without bothering about the principles.[9]

The weakness of this approach is that it does not resolve challenges raised by the Platonic dialogues themselves. (A further consideration, which I leave aside for the moment, is that without accepting the Theory of Principles as a commitment throughout Plato's philosophical career, it becomes difficult to understand the attempts made in the Old Academy – particularly by Plato's immediate successors, Speusippus and Xenocrates – to move from Plato the philosopher to Platonism the philosophical system.)[10] These challenges suggest that many dialogues were written with the contents of the Unwritten Doctrines in mind; Plato regularly hints that there is a superior approach to the problem under discussion which is not going to be immediately revealed. If this superior approach is understanding the principles via dialectic (only hinted at in the dialogues), this would make it a central feature of Plato's thought, rather than a late and peripheral development.

The most significant of these challenges is raised by Plato's own criticism of writing at *Phdr.* 274c–277a. On the face of it, this seems like a strange criticism to emanate from such an accomplished writer. It has been widely claimed that this is why Plato chose the dialogue form (rather than a philosophical treatise or poetry) and that his own writings are exempt from this criticism since they recreate (or mimic) orality.[11] But is this really the case? One of the criticisms of

---

[8] For example, *Physics* 209b, cited earlier in this section, which simply concerns a divergence between Plato's views discussed within the Academy and as expressed in the *Timaeus*.
[9] Cf. the discussion at Hösle 2019: 335–336.   [10] Cf. Dillon 2003: 16–22; Gerson 2013.
[11] It should be noted, though, that the philosophical treatise as a distinct genre developed only with Aristotle.

writing raised in the *Phaedrus* is that a written text always says the same thing, and sadly – even if we can regularly gain new insights by repeated reading – this holds true for Plato's dialogues also. Similarly, a written text cannot choose the reader that is appropriate to it, but is accessible to everyone, even those incapable of fully understanding it; Plato's works are not exempt from this either.

The *Phaedrus*' criticism of writing is not an aberration. Rather, it is only one of a number of passages within the dialogues themselves that explicitly state or imply that there is a better way to achieve philosophical insight, rather than simply reading philosophy books (even those of Plato)! These so-called deliberate gaps (see Section 2) reveal that Plato, the author, and Socrates know more on specific topics (specifically the issues addressed by the Unwritten Doctrines) than they are prepared to say. The silence is explained either because Socrates' interlocutor (suggesting the reader too) would not be capable of following or because the only way to approach these insights (via oral teaching or via dialectic more specifically) necessarily cannot be replicated by means of a written text. These deliberate gaps are found across such a wide range of Plato's dialogues (e.g. *Rep.* 506d2–507a2, 509c1–509c11; *Tim.* 48c2–48e1) that it becomes untenable to simply dismiss them as marginal to Plato's thought. The explicit concealment of knowledge actually forms a significant recurring motif across the corpus.[12]

Another noteworthy document for advancing the claims of Plato's Unwritten Doctrines is the *Seventh Letter*, the authenticity of which is disputed. While I shall consider the evidence for a Theory of Principles in the *Seventh Letter* (341b1–345c3) in Section 2, it is clear that one does not need to rely on this text (or indeed solely on the testimonia) in order to advance the cause of the Unwritten Doctrines. Rather, similar commitments are indicated in various ways within the dialogues themselves. Even if the principles are not so explicitly treated in the dialogues, the *Philebus* comes close to expounding them (see Section 3).

1.3 The Tübingen School

This particular interpretative approach – the attribution of Unwritten Doctrines to Plato, assigning them a particularly central role in his thought and the resulting emphasis on the Theory of Principles – has become primarily associated with small pockets of southern Germany (the Tübingen School) and northern Italy. The inaugural work was Hans Joachim Krämer's (1929–2015) *Arete bei Platon und Aristoteles* (*Virtue in Plato and Aristotle*, 1959), followed by Konrad Gaiser's (1929–1988) *Platons ungeschriebene Lehre* (*Plato's Unwritten Doctrine*, 1963).

---

[12] Szlezák 1999: 9–11 examines the extent to which this explicit concealment defines the *Euthydemus*.

Another highly influential volume was Thomas Szlezák's (1940–2023) *Platon lesen* (1993; *Reading Plato*, 1999). Other important scholars from the Tübingen School include Jens Halfwassen (1958–2020) at Heidelberg and Vittorio Hösle (born 1960) at Notre Dame. The influential work of Giovanni Reale (1931–2014) has led to the partial adoption of the term *Tübingen–Milan School*. The Tübingen–Milan School is actually less geographically restricted than its name might suggest – spreading, for example, via Reale's student, Maurizio Migliori (1943–2023), who taught for many years at Macerata, as well as via Reale's influence in Latin America, supported by the translations of his works into Spanish, such as his volumes with Dario Antiseri, *Historia de la filosofía* (by Juan Andrés Iglesias, Maria Pons Irazazábal, and Antoni Martínez Riu).[13] Additionally, Reale's *Toward a New Interpretation of Plato* (1997) made his views accessible in North America.[14]

While the scholars of the Tübingen School present an original interpretation of Plato, it should not be seen as a break in the continuity of Platonic scholarship: claims of Plato's oral teaching can be found in Dietrich Tiedemann (1748–1803), Wilhelm Gottlieb Tennemann (1761–1819), and (outside the German tradition) Léon Robin (1866–1947).

It is not my objective to provide a detailed analysis of the contributions of each individual scholar of the Tübingen School. Indeed, certain views often associated with the Tübingen School have been developed or adopted by scholars outside this area, notably John Niemeyer Findlay (1974) and Lloyd Gerson (2013; 2014). My aim is primarily to clarify the difficulties which the Tübingen scholars (and earlier Platonists) identified in interpreting Plato's legacy and to examine the merits of the solutions which they propose. Whether or not we accept their conclusions, we still have to respond to the same challenges of interpretation. First, Plato can be a difficult philosopher to pin down; he chose to leave us a corpus consisting largely of dialogues[15] and clearly not every view expressed in the dialogues is Plato's.[16] Second, although Plato was an accomplished literary craftsman, several passages in the dialogues hint at (or explicitly argue for) a more thorough approach for reaching philosophical insight than that contained within the dialogues themselves.

The history of Platonic scholarship can be viewed as consisting of two interpretative methodologies: the 'Protestant' approach, which sees the dialogues as the sole authority for Plato's thought (*sola scriptura* – the text alone interpreted

---

[13] On Migliori's allegiance to the Tübingen–Milan School, see Migliori 2023: 9.

[14] Translation of the 1991 (tenth) Italian edition; see Reale 1997 and 2010.

[15] There are some exceptions: the *Apology* is presented as Socrates' defence speeches; the philosophical content of the *Timaeus* is delivered in the form of a monologue.

[16] An obvious example is Thrasymachus' claim at *Rep.* I 338c that justice is the interest of the stronger, which is subsequently refuted.

by means of the text itself, *sui ipsius interpres*), and the 'Catholic' approach, which regards the entire Platonic tradition (including the testimonia which we find in Aristotle concerning Plato and the Old Academy) as a valid source of further evidence.[17] Nowadays, the fissure between these methodologies tends to follow linguistic rather than confessional lines: the Romantic approach of Schleiermacher, who, as a theologian, drew upon the methodology of Protestant biblical hermeneutics in his interpretation of Plato became (via Paul Shorey (1857–1934), Harold Cherniss (1904–1987), and Gregory Vlastos (1907–1991))[18] the dominant paradigm in the Anglo-American world.[19] From the alternative perspective of the Tübingen School's approach, once we decide to take seriously the possibility that Plato presented his core philosophical views outside of the dialogues, we then need to find a means to approach this philosophical core (e.g. through the testimonia). For this reason, we should not think that the Tübingen School subordinates the dialogues (Plato's actual writings) in favour of approaching Plato via the comments of a somewhat disgruntled former student, Aristotle (as is sometimes portrayed in the scholarship of its rivals). Rather, it adopts the testimonia on Plato's Unwritten Doctrines as a legitimate response to Plato's own comments within the dialogues.

If Plato's view of the higher core of philosophical knowledge was dealt with outside the dialogues, this leads to the question of what function the dialogues themselves served (since, in this case, it would clearly not be the transmission of higher philosophical knowledge). The dialogues could be regarded as exoteric, intended for use by a broader public outside the Academy, while the Unwritten Doctrines would be esoteric, revealed to an inner core within the Academy itself.

This Tübingen claim of 'esotericism' is often portrayed negatively and unfairly.[20] Our modern understanding of knowledge is that it should be made public, although other societies prefer to keep knowledge secret as the source of power (e.g. the Eleusinian Mysteries in Plato's day). Yet Plato's Unwritten Doctrines – both the fact that they existed and the content of the Theory of Principles – were not actively concealed. Furthermore, the esotericism claimed by the Tübingen School is often unfairly confounded with the esotericism

---

[17] Krämer 1990: 14–16; Gerson 2014: 397–398.
[18] For example, Cherniss 1944 – although earlier than the first Tübingen School work: Krämer 1959 – and Cherniss 1945, as well as Vlastos 1963, a review of Krämer 1959. Shorey 1903 is strongly Schleiermachean and Cherniss was famously presented as a half-Schleiermacher (*Schleiermacher dimidiatus*); cf. Krämer 1990: 37. For context on the approaches of Shorey and Cherniss (as Anglo-American unitarians) and Vlastos (reading across sections of dialogues), see Gill 2002: 147–156.
[19] Cf. Gerson 2014: 399–401; Szlezák 2019a: 499–500 and 2021: 496–497.
[20] Vlastos 1963: 654 presents the Unwritten Doctrines as crediting Plato 'with a private (and secret!) philosophy meant to supersede the one which he published in the dialogues'.

propounded by Leo Strauss (1899–1973):[21] the notion that the Platonic texts have both an exoteric meaning and a hidden esoteric one (only accessible to Strauss and his followers).[22]

The Tübingen School does not argue for esotericism in the sense of 'hidden' or 'secret', but rather distinguishes between Plato's exoteric productions in the sense of writings which were intended for a broader readership, including those outside the Academy and his esoteric activity: his oral teaching for his own students within the Academy itself. It is for this reason that Tübingen School publications often refer to 'inner-Academic' activity rather than to 'esotericism' to avoid being confounded with Straussian esotericism.[23] The dialogues were probably intended for distinct groups of readers: as a mnemonic for members of the Academy who had already been exposed to the Theory of Principles (as suggested by *Phdr.* 278a), as well as fulfilling a protreptic or hortatory function among the broader public, encouraging it to turn to the study of Platonic philosophy.[24]

The testimonia are of varying significance. They can be broadly categorised into three groups: (1) Plato's 'self-testimonies' (*Phdr.* 274b6–278e3; *Prt.* 356e8–357c1; *Meno* 76e3–77b1; *Phd.* 107b4–107b10; *Rep.* VI 506d2–507a2; *Rep.* VI 509c1–509c11; *Parm.* 136d4–136e3; *Soph.* 254b7–254d3; *Plt.* 284a1–284e8; *Tim.* 48c2–48e1; *Tim.* 54c4–54d7; *Laws* X 894a1–894a5);[25] (2) the testimonia of Aristotle (*Physics* 209b11–209b17, 209b33–210a2; *NE* 1095a30–1095b3; *Met.* 1018b37–1019a4, 1054a20–1054a32, 1061a10–1061a15, 1091b13–1091b15; *EE* 1218a15–1218a28); as well as (3) testimonia from commentators on Aristotle (Alexander of Aphrodisias, Aristoxenus, Sextus Empiricus, Simplicius).[26]

The varying reliability of the testimonia presents one challenge to the Tübingen School; there are others. It is not my objective here to account for why the Tübingen School approach has met with limited success in Anglo-American scholarship, although I shall briefly outline some significant obstacles which it faced.

1. The ascent of the Schleiermachean approach to Plato (via the dialogues rather than the tradition) occurred at major North American universities: Chicago, Johns Hopkins, UC Berkeley, and Princeton.[27] The two scholars

---

[21] Hösle 2019: 345n55.
[22] E.g. an exoteric reading of the *Republic* is that philosophers should become kings, whereas the esoteric Straussian reading is that Plato did not view this as feasible. Cf. Strauss 2000.
[23] One of the major concerns with Strauss' approach is his use of non-philosophical keys to decode philosophical dialogues. Cf. Gerson 2014: 398n2.
[24] Szlezák 1999: 20 argues for the possibility of three separate groups of addressees.
[25] Krämer 1990 categorises *Epist.* VII 340b1–345c3 as a self-testimony.
[26] These are all contained in Krämer 1990, although I depart slightly from his categorisation.
[27] I distinguish the Schleiermacheans from the broader spectrum of anti-esoteric approaches; see Section 5.1.

dominant in North America at the time, Cherniss and Vlastos, were (at best) dismissive of the concept of the Unwritten Doctrines, which rendered it acceptable to ignore the problems that the Tübingen School emphasised (see Section 5). Krämer's groundbreaking 1959 study was dismissed by Vlastos;[28] this lent support not so much to attempts to refute his views, but – of far greater concern – simply ignoring them altogether.[29] Vlastos' significance for the dismissal of Krämer's work is illustrated by Krämer's response to Vlastos' *Gnomon* review, which itself triggered another negative response from Vlastos.

2. On a practical level, most of the significant Tübingen–Milan works were published either in German or Italian and there has been relatively little available in English.[30] This certainly accounts for its limited diffusion across the Anglosphere, but does not fully explain it. Findlay, for example, independently addressed similar issues in his English-language monograph.[31]

3. Beyond the arguments drawn from Plato, the Tübingen School approach utilises an understanding of ancient mathematics, as well as an interpretation of the history of philosophy which is indebted to German Idealism; culturally, this is a reading of philosophy which is more intuitive for many German scholars.[32] Yet we must consider to what extent other approaches actually respond better to the challenges raised by the Tübingen School than the notion of Plato's Unwritten Doctrines does and how much is simply based on cultural or academic preferences which cannot be defended from Plato's own texts.

Sextus Empiricus' report is particularly contentious since the Tübingen School claims it as evidence for the Theory of Principles which is independent of Aristotle, an assertion denied by Vlastos.[33] Additionally, Vlastos objected to Aristotle's reliability as a witness and the claim that the *Phaedrus*' criticism of writing applies to Plato's own work.[34] Furthermore, Vlastos attempted to downplay the significance of the Theory of Principles. Consider Aristoxenus' report of Plato's oral teaching on the Principles, his disastrous and ill-fated lecture (or lectures; see Section 5.3) on the Good:

---

[28] Vlastos 1963 and 1973.   [29] Gerson 2014: 400 attests to Vlastos' negative influence.
[30] The situation is changing: e.g. Krämer 1990; Reale 1997; Szlezák 1999; Nikulin 2012b; Gerson 2014; Hösle 2019; Migliori 2020 and 2023; Halfwassen 2021; O'Brien 2021a and 2021b.
[31] Findlay 1974.
[32] For example, Halfwassen's reading of the Theory of Principles allows for a greater continuity between Plato, Speusippus, Plotinian Neoplatonism, and Hegel. Cf. Section 4 and Halfwassen 2021.
[33] Cf. Vlastos 1963: 643. Szlezák 2021: 518 suggests that it indicates the structure of Plato's lecture(s) *On the Good*.
[34] Cf. Hösle 2019: 342–343.

Just as Aristotle was accustomed to say, the majority of those hearing Plato's lectures *On the Good* experienced the following: For each one used to come, supposing that he would be informed about one of those things considered human goods, such as riches, health or strength ... But when the lectures appeared to be about Mathematics and Numbers and Geometry and Astronomy and Limit, that the Good is one, it appeared to them to be a complete paradox. Some – I think – looked down on the matter and others criticised it.[35]

Vlastos argued that this ill-fated display was a once-off event, rather than representative of Plato's regular teaching, which has the effect of marginalising it. This does not agree, though, with the evidence of several dialogues which strongly suggest a theory which Plato was not prepared to expound at length there, and with the testimonia of Aristotle which indicate that this theory is the Theory of Principles. In Section 5, I shall examine the chief arguments advanced against the Tübingen School more closely and evaluate their cogency. As Hösle points out, though, much of the opposition to the Tübingen interpretation really stems from the anachronistic assumption that oral teaching necessarily precedes written publication (as is often the case in the modern academic tradition).[36] This was not the case in Plato's Athens, which was in the course of transition from orality to increasing reliance upon literacy. Plato's disastrous lecture(s) on the Good remind(s) us why – even if the oral teachings were not actively concealed – he would have been averse to broadcasting them more widely to a general public, lacking both the necessary philosophical preparation to benefit from them and a mindset sympathetic to his claims.[37] It is for this reason that the Theory of Principles is only hinted at in the dialogues, but not clearly expounded, since writing is inadequate to enable this level of philosophical ascent.

The issue of esotericism is also relevant for evaluating the nature and status of the dialogues. That Plato regularly thematises the existence of unwritten doctrines is a clear sign that the principles should not be considered as a marginal aspect of his thought and, like the lecture(s) on the Good, highlights the distinction between esotericism and active concealment.[38] Plato's adoption of the dialogue form is often presented as an attempt to avoid explicitly revealing his views. However, as Szlezák notes, there is a distinction between composing

---

[35] Aristoxenus, *The Elements of Harmony* II (pp. 39–40 Da Rios = *TP* 7 Gaiser).
[36] Hösle 2019: 343.
[37] This is illustrated by the accessibility of written texts to even unsuitable readers at *Phdr.* 275e, the inability of written texts to adequately teach the truth at *Phdr.* 276c9, reflected in the warning against the premature revelation of philosophical insights at *Laws* XII 968e4–968e5 since it will not lead to understanding, and the attack on Dionysius' breech of etiquette in revealing the principles at *Epist.* VII 341d.
[38] Szlezák 1999: 85–86.

dialogues and anonymity.[39] Publishing under a pseudonym was an option available to Plato if he had wished to distance himself completely from his written works. Just because Plato adopted the dialogue form does not mean that it is impossible to attribute specific doctrines to him; Szlezák mentions the immortality of the soul as an example.[40]

1.4 The Consequences of the Theory of Principles for Later Platonism

Much work by later members of the Tübingen School (notably Halfwassen) extended the insights of the Theory of Principles to subsequent Platonism (such as the Old Academy and Neoplatonism). The very name 'Neoplatonism' suggests a break – perhaps even a radical break – from the phases of Platonism which preceded it. Yet this term is a fairly recent one in the history of Platonic scholarship.[41] The 'Neoplatonists' did not apply this label to themselves. If one accepts that Plato posited a Theory of Principles and further accepts the absolute transcendence of the First Principle, a feature which comes across at *Rep.* VI 509b and which his nephew Speusippus also insisted upon,[42] then the Tübingen School's approach in assigning a particular centrality to the metaphysics of the One (or henology, a discourse about the One) leads to regarding Plato and Plotinus as being in almost complete agreement (see Section 4).[43] (Although it is beyond the scope of this Element, the Tübingen School also displays a marked tendency to stress the continuity between Plotinian Neoplatonism and German Idealism, particularly the Idealism of Georg Wilhelm Friedrich Hegel.)[44]

1.5 The Significance of the Theory of Principles

My aim in this Element is less to argue for the adoption of the Tübingen School approach in preference to Schleiermachean or other anti-esoteric interpretations, but rather to focus on the issues at stake in determining whether we opt for one approach or the other: issues which have to be addressed whether we accept the Tübingen School views or not. While the Schleiermachean interpretation has addressed issues within the dialogues themselves, the Tübingen School has also thematised questions that go beyond the dialogues, the answers to which radically affect our understanding of Plato. Even if we choose to reject the evidence of the *Seventh Letter* or the testimonia, we still need to consider the

---

[39] Szlezák 1999: 17 refers to the example of Søren Kierkegaard, who did, in fact, publish some works under pseudonyms for the sake of anonymity.
[40] Szlezák 1999: 17.   [41] The first usage is generally traced to Büsching 1774.
[42] Based on the testimony of Aristotle, *Met.* 1092a14–1092a15.   [43] Halfwassen 2006: 423.
[44] Krämer 1990: 157–167; Halfwassen 2015: 331.

original readership for which the dialogues were intended, the relationship of the dialogues to Plato's teaching within the Academy and how we should read the dialogues in the light of Plato's own comments, made repeatedly throughout his corpus, on the deficiency of writing as a mechanism for achieving or transmitting philosophical insight and his continued insistence on a superior way of achieving this: the 'longer and greater road' (*Rep.* IV 435d3) of dialectic.[45] The immense merit of the Tübingen approach is that it offers solutions to meet all of these challenges.

2 Plato's Criticism of Writing

2.1 Plato's Own Comments ('Self-Testimonies') on Writing

Plato's most famous comments on writing are found in his criticism of writing (sometimes known as the *Schriftkritik*) at *Phaedrus* 274b–278e.[46] The god Theuth is roundly criticised by his fellow god and king of Egypt, Thamus, for his invention of writing:

> You have not discovered a drug of remembrance but of reminding and you provide your students *not with true wisdom, but with the reputation of wisdom, for having 'learned' much without instruction, they will seem sagacious when the majority of them are ignorant and hard to bear, since they pretend to be wise, but are not wise.* (275a5–275b2; my italics)

At *Prot.* 328e5–329b1, similar reservations regarding the inability of orators to answer questions, just like books, are raised. Does this criticism of writing apply even to Plato's dialogues (which is of significance for understanding Plato's relationship to his own writings) or does it exclusively target the writing of others? If this criticism does apply, then why did Plato compose written texts, if writing is so deficient for philosophical instruction, and for whom? Plato's criticism of writing is not merely a general one – although many aspects of his criticism are applicable to all types of writing – but specifically focuses on its use to someone who wishes to please God – that is, the philosopher (*Phdr.* 274b9).[47]

Three principal lines of argumentation are available to those who wish to deny that Plato's criticism applies to his own texts:

---

[45] It is, of course, possible to regard the *Seventh Letter* as spurious and still accept that Plato posited a Theory of Principles.

[46] Although this Element discusses the problems addressed by the Tübingen School approach, rather than focusing on the contributions of individual scholars, the insights treated in this section are indebted primarily to the work of Thomas Alexander Szlezák.

[47] Szlezák 1999: 31. Szlezák's detailed philological analysis (2019a: 411–413) has rendered this claim null and void.

1. The term Plato uses for the texts which he criticises, σύγγραμμα, is presented as referring to a treatise, and not a dialogue.[48] Yet in the *Phaedrus*' Egyptian tale, Thamus criticises the τέχνη (art or skill) of writing (274c8–274d2); Szlezák highlights this focus on the 'art' of writing as a whole, not one particular genre of writing (which would open up the claim that the dialogue is somehow an exempt form).[49] The *Phaedrus* draws a distinction between oral and written 'speech', not different literary genres.[50] Socrates on four occasions notes that the criticism applies to all forms of writing (258d, 277d, 277e, 278b–278c).[51]
2. As it is particularly remarkable for a criticism such as this to stem from a dialogue of Plato's middle period, when he had already produced quite a considerable corpus of written texts, Schleiermacher attempted a radical alternative chronology, locating the *Phaedrus* in Plato's earlier period (although Schleiermacher privileged the content of the dialogues when forming internal connections between the constituent components of the corpus).[52] This would evoke an author who had doubts about writing early in his career, marginalising this criticism of writing. The same argumentation is applied to the Theory of Principles also, placing it towards the end of Plato's career, thereby again marginalising it. In fact, both the Theory of Principles and the criticism of writing are central to Plato's thought and are regularly and repeatedly thematised across Plato's corpus. They are also interrelated. (It is often – although not exclusively – the full details of his Theory of Principles which Plato refuses to outline explicitly in his corpus, although he regularly hints at the existence of this theory.)
3. The dialogue form replicates orality and, as a result, evades the deficiencies of the written word. Yet even Plato's works do not escape the problems which he identifies as intrinsic to writing. Leaving aside the criticism that writing serves as a substitute for wisdom, is little more than a mnemonic aid, and produces people who are difficult to get along with, Plato advances three substantial difficulties with writing:

    1. The text always says the same thing (*Phdr.* 275d4–275d9).
    2. It is incapable of choosing its reader (*Phdr.* 275e2–275e3).
    3. It is unable to defend itself from attacks, needing support from its 'father' – that is, its author (*Phdr.* 275e3–275e5). It is not an ideally crafted text that escapes these deficiencies, but dialectic (conducted orally). 'The word written with knowledge in the soul of the one who

---

[48] Szlezák has repeated pointed out the fallacy of this line of argumentation, since Plato criticises γραφή in general, rather than the σύγγραμμα in particular. Cf. Szlezák 2019a: 411.
[49] Szlezák 1985: 8. [50] Szlezák 1985: 10. [51] Rowe 1986: 114. [52] Taylor 2002: 74.

understands, which can defend itself, knowing to whom it should speak, and before whom it must be silent' (*Phdr.* 276a5–276a7) does not refer to the Platonic dialogue, but to 'the living and ensouled word of the one who knows, of which the inscribed word may with reason be called the image', the 'legitimate brother' of writing (*Phdr.* 276a8–276a9) – that is, the oral teaching of the dialectician. Furthermore, if there were genres which constitute exceptions to this criticism of writing, such as dialogues, then one can easily envisage a situation with so many excepted genres that the criticism itself becomes pointless.[53]

Most significant of all, though, Plato himself tells us that his criticism of writing applies to his own texts. At *Phdr.* 276b1–277a5, a widely misunderstood passage,[54] Plato notes that the clever farmer would avoid sowing the seeds which he values and from which he expects a good harvest in some garden of Adonis. This is clearly a reference to the philosopher who avoids committing his best ideas to writing if he expects a good harvest; the image, though, has been rather obscured by the reference to the garden of Adonis. This refers to a religious rite in which grain seeds would be sown in clay bowls and kept in the heat and dark for a few days to allow for quick growth (but the resulting plant produces no seed). Szlezák argues that just as the clever farmer would not sow all of his seeds in the garden of Adonis since this would deprive him of the possibility of reaping a harvest, so too the dialectician does not 'sow' all of his knowledge in his writings where it would fail to bear fruit.[55] If he were to do this, it would be for the sake of the religious festival or for play (as in the case of the author of a philosophical text).[56]

While opponents of the Tübingen School are typically dismissive of the *Phaedrus' Schriftkritik*, Mary Margaret Mackenzie (1982) and Christopher Rowe (1986) have taken it seriously. Although I think that the Tübingen interpretation has the most to commend it since it accounts for the deliberate gaps, Mackenzie regards the *Schriftkritik* as an antinomy – that is, it has the same status as the phrase 'I am lying', which, if true, must be false and vice versa.[57] In the same manner, Mackenzie regards the claim advanced at *Phdr.* 277e7–277e8 that 'No logos has ever been composed, either in metre or without metre, that is worthy of high esteem' as an antinomy: a written text which repudiates written texts.[58] She sees Plato employing dialectic as a literary

---

[53] Szlelzák 1985: 359; cf. Reale 2010: 92–93.
[54] For this type of misunderstanding, cf. Hackforth 1952: 159 suggesting that the plants will bear fine fruit in eight days.
[55] Szlezák 2019a: 414–415.   [56] Reale 2010: 82.
[57] From Euboulides the Dialectician; Diogenes Laertius 2.108. Cf. Mackenzie 1982: 64.
[58] Mackenzie 1982: 65 also links this passage with claims of 'esoteric doctrines'.

device which masks the real dialectical engagement with the reader.⁵⁹ Plato's dismissal of writing can be seen both as drawing attention to the process of dialectic and, by outraging us, as confirming the power of the written word.⁶⁰

Rowe's solution is to regard the *Phaedrus* as a sustained *apologia*; just like Socrates' attitude to the myth of Boreas and Oreithyia (229b–230a), the reader should not actively disbelieve Plato's works, but, at the same time, should not expect more from them than they can deliver.⁶¹ The responses of both Mackenzie and Rowe have significantly more merit than Schleiermacher's misguided attempt to avoid the problems that the *Schriftkritik* causes by creatively dating the *Phaedrus* as an early work.

Part of the difficulty is that there is a strong tendency to view the dialogues through the frame of our own understanding of literacy, regarding them as equivalent to the latest research paper outlining the state of the art in the field, reflecting views developed through lectures and oral discussion in the Academy. This imposes our contemporary research culture, in which literacy trumps orality, onto Plato. Literacy was less dominant in classical Athens and was only coming to the fore in Plato's day; his critique in the *Phaedrus* can be read as wariness towards a new development. The situation is complex, though, due to the distinction between prose and verse works – although here too Plato is something of a trailblazer in composing philosophical prose, rather than expressing his insights in verse.⁶² Furthermore, the performative aspect of poetry complicates the distinction between reading and listening.⁶³

Plato himself emphasises a different scale of values. The philosopher is capable of producing 'more valuable things' (τιμιώτερα, *Phdr.* 278d8) than what is revealed in his writings.⁶⁴ What does Plato mean when he states that something is 'more valuable'? Szlezák suggests that 'more valuable' means closer to the principle(s), a definition which Plato has already presented at *Phdr.* 234e–236b when the criteria for a better speech on Eros than that of Lysias are outlined – the better speech is that containing superior philosophical content (although it could be claimed that 'superior' might have another interpretation such as 'more effective at producing virtue').⁶⁵ This is stressed by Reale, who notes that writing, as it is depicted in Plato, implies 'play', while orality is used to evoke an element of seriousness.⁶⁶ This is largely because writing does not

---

⁵⁹ Mackenzie 1982: 69.   ⁶⁰ Mackenzie 1982: 72.   ⁶¹ Rowe 1986: 120.
⁶² There is some Presocratic philosophical prose; cf. Osborne 1998: 28.
⁶³ This performative aspect is also found in Plato's dialogues; as Goldhill 2002: 90 notes, Socrates' commitment to virtue in the *Phaedo* is performed, rather than advanced by argument.
⁶⁴ Cf. Reale 2010: 89–91.
⁶⁵ Szlezák 2019a: 415–416. Cf. Reale 2010: 91: it is the principles which are 'more valuable'.
⁶⁶ Reale 2010: 77.

allow the reader to attain insights independently, but only serves as a reminder of those that have already been attained.

When Plato refers to writing as an image (*Phdr.* 275d–275e), this is intended in a negative manner: 'Phaedrus, writing and painting have something marvellously strange in common. The offspring of painting stand as if alive, but if you question them, they are pompously silent. (Written) words are the same' (*Phdr.* 275d4–275d7). This paves the way for Plato's criticism of writing always saying the same thing; just like a painting it remains fixed. (Similarly the author of *Epist.* VII notes that 'no one with intelligence will dare to commit his serious thoughts to it, especially in an immutable form, as is the case with written impressions', 343a1–343a3.) It highlights the level of deficiency exhibited when Socrates in the *Republic* can only pursue his discussion of the Good in terms of images.

2.2 The Theory and Hierarchy of Forms

Often regarded as the most characteristic of Plato's doctrines, the Theory of Forms is vital to understanding his conception of reality.[67] Since this theory is relevant to the Theory of Principles, as well as to our understanding of the nature of images (relevant for how Plato conceives of writing as an image of orality) and for evaluating the philosophical digression of the *Seventh Letter*, which is a key text for the Tübingen School approach, a brief excursus is in order. Plato posited two realms: the sense-perceptible world and an intelligible realm consisting of abstract, changeless entities, Ideas or Forms (although these entities should not be regarded as existing in space or time). The Form (*eidos*) of Beauty can be viewed as the paradigm[68] and 'perfect exemplar' of Beauty.[69] Its beauty is more 'real' than the beauty of a beautiful woman or object of art and is what makes this beauty possible.

There is a hierarchy among Forms: Plato also draws a distinction between Form-Numbers or 'logico-mathematical' Forms (e.g. the Form of Three of which every example of three in our realm is merely an instantiation) and Forms corresponding to value (e.g. beauty, justice, etc.)[70] The highest of all Forms, according to the *Republic*, is the Form (or Idea) of the Good (often identified with the One).[71] For this reason understanding the Theory of Forms is

---

[67] For a more detailed introduction to this theory, see Sedley 2016. While seen as essentially Platonic, there may have been Pythagorean antecedents, cf. Aristotle *Met.* 987a29–987a30.
[68] Cf. *Euthyphro* 6e on the Form of piety.   [69] Sedley 2016: 3.   [70] Sedley 2016: 15.
[71] The argument might be made that there is not a single, consistent hierarchy of Forms across the dialogues: the highest Form examined and the object of ascent in the *Symposium* is the Beautiful (see Section 3.3) and the 'greatest kinds' in the *Sophist* are Being, Same, Different, Change, and Rest.

of significance when attempting to comprehend the Theory of Principles, although, unfortunately, referring to the Idea of the Good can lead one to see it as just another Form and mask its radical otherness (discussed in Section 3).

There are numerous difficulties of interpretation with the Theory of Forms (one of these being the possibility that Plato abandoned it later in life). A key problem concerns the range of the Forms – that is, of what things are there Forms? There are Forms of natural kinds (like Human and Horse), Forms of Numbers, and Forms of properties (like largeness and smallness), but as Plato's Parmenides asks the young Socrates, are there Forms of any 'dishonourable and worthless thing'?[72] While Socrates answers that there are not, this is a young and intellectually naive Socrates who prompts the response from the more philosophically sophisticated Parmenides that he shall one day outgrow his reservation, although it is difficult to interpret this remark, as Socrates expresses doubt about a Form of Human just before (*Parm.* 130c1–130c4). However, if there is a Form of Bee, as suggested at *Meno* 72a8–72b2, then there must surely be a Form of Human.[73] As outlined at Section 2.3, this difficulty concerning the exact range of Forms plays a role in whether we should accept the *Seventh Letter* as authentic or not (which in turn influences how we respond to this document as a source for Plato's Unwritten Doctrines).

One of the difficulties (philosophically) with the views expounded by Cherniss in particular is that in rejecting the Idea of the Good's superordinate role, Plato's metaphysics appear to rest upon nothing more than a collection of disconnected Forms. This is related to the attempt to portray the Idea of the Good as either simply another Form or presenting it as the sum of the (other) Forms (again denying its radical transcendence and attempting to undermine its identification with a principle, the One, as well as the claim at *Rep.* VI 509b that it is 'beyond Being').[74] It is because the Good provides the other Forms with intelligibility that they become boniform (or 'good-like').[75] The attempt to avoid the content of Plato's Unwritten Doctrines undermines not just his epistemology, then, but also his metaphysics since the Forms would consequently lack any kind of unifying coherence.

Evidently, claims that the Good is the sum of the Forms is a recognition of this objection and an attempt to forestall it. Schleiermacheans who adopt this approach rely on the *Sophist* (e.g. *Sophist* 251a–259d).[76] So Cherniss argues

---

[72] *Parm.* 130c6–130c7; cf. *Soph.* 249a and Aristotle's comments at *Met.* 1074b17–1074b18.
[73] Sedley 2016: 19 suggests that Plato (at least when writing the *Parmenides*) did indeed intend to expand the range of Forms.
[74] See Gerson 2014: 403.   [75] Gerson 2014: 407.
[76] Cherniss 1944: 46–47; Cherniss 1945: 97n118 also appeals to the authority of Aristotle (e.g. *Met.* 1075b17–1075b20), although Cherniss rejects Aristotle's authority as a commentator on Plato elsewhere (as at Cherniss 1944: 177, 258). Cf. Krämer 1990: 36.

that Being is just a type of Idea that communicates with other Ideas (or Forms), like Different, Same, Change, and Rest, but it does not have the sort of relation to the other Ideas that the Ideas have to the particulars[77] and maintains that what is true for these five Ideas is true for the others (claiming support from *Sophist* 254c).[78] It might be possible to construct some sort of argument opposed to a hierarchical relationship of the Forms based on the 'third man' argument of the *Parmenides*, where the justification for positing a Form over its instantiations might be used to posit a Form above this Form and lead to an infinite regress, but this is not the argument that Cherniss makes. In any case, this argument is not valid against the relationship between the Forms and the Idea of the Good as their principle, which would seem to rule out the indefinite postulation of increasingly higher principles.[79]

In *Republic* X, Socrates uses the example of the bed to refer to three levels of reality: the least real is the image of a bed painted by an artist (which is not even a bed at all). The next level up would be any bed made by a craftsman, which is inferior to the Idea or Form of the Bed which every craftsman has in mind when turning to make a bed. As the 'perfect exemplar' of the bed due to which each physical instantiation of the bed owes its existence, it is clear that this bed is superior (or 'prior') to the beds at the two lower levels. This deficiency of images is key to understanding Plato's own treatment of the Good in the *Republic* and the way he flags the degree to which his written account necessarily falls short of oral instruction.

2.3 References to an Oral Teaching: *Seventh Letter* (340b1–345c3)

One of the grounds for attacking the Tübingen School approach is its employment of the *Seventh Letter* as evidence for an oral teaching of Plato's. This document has been transmitted to us as a work of Plato's, although many scholars (particularly in the English-speaking world and partly as the legacy of Shorey and Cherniss there) regard it as spurious.[80] A major difficulty is that the *Seventh Letter* postulates Forms of artefacts[81] – or Ideas of artificial

---

[77] Cherniss 1945: 53–54. I use the term ' Ideas' rather than 'Forms' here to follow Cherniss' practice.

[78] Cherniss 1944: 46.

[79] *Parm.* 132a1–132b1, 132d1–133a3; see Gerson 2005: 228. Fine 1993: 203–204 discusses the third man argument in detail.

[80] Krämer 1990: 36.

[81] Other grounds for rejecting Plato as an author are the references to an evil divinity at 326e and 336b (Burnyeat 2015: ix) and claims of philosophical incompetence (Burnyeat 2015: 122). For a response to many of Burnyeat's arguments, see Politis 2020, who has demonstrated the value of the *Seventh Letter* independent of the question of its authenticity.

things – which runs counter to the testimony of Aristotle that Plato postulated only Forms of natural things:[82]

> The form of house does not exist in this way, unless the art [of house-building] exists separately (and there is not generation and destruction of these, but the house without its matter and health and all the objects of art exist and do not exist in another manner); but, if it does, only for objects of nature. Therefore Plato did not speak badly when he said there are as many Forms as there are things in nature, if really there are Forms, except for things such as fire, flesh, head, for all of these are matter and the last matter is that which is most especially substance. (*Met.* 1070a14–1070a20; cf. *Met.* 991b6–991b7, 1080a5–1080a6)[83]

However, Plato certainly employs the imagery of Forms of artefacts when he discusses the Form of a bed at *Rep.* X 597c–597d or the Form of a shuttle at *Cra.* 389a7–389a8; cf. *Gorgias* 503e).[84] *Epist.* VII 342d2–342d6 runs counter to the testimony of Aristotle in claiming Forms of artefacts: 'The same is true of straight and curved shapes and of colours, of the Good and of the Beautiful and of the just and of all bodies *whether generated artificially or in accordance with nature*, of fire, of water and of all such things, of all living beings and of all dispositions in the soul, of all actions and affections' (my emphasis). It is difficult to imagine that Aristotle would claim that Plato did not posit Forms of artefacts if this was not the case (since such a false statement would have been easily exposed).[85]

Politis sounds a warning: 'There is reason not to allow the *Seventh Letter* to dictate one's reading of Plato, irrespective of the issue of authenticity.'[86] I shall not make use of what Burnyeat characterises as the 'lazy solution' that the *Seventh Letter* may have been composed by an associate of Plato's at the Academy during his lifetime or shortly after his death.[87] However, since there

---

[82] At *Parm.* 130c5–130c7, the Young Socrates rules out 'things that might appear ridiculous, like hair and mud and filth or any other such dishonourable and worthless thing', although he is unsure if there is a Form of fire and water and does not mention Forms of artefacts.
[83] However, it should be noted that Aristotle uses artefacts against the Platonists and exploits Plato's own inconsistencies; cf. Papandreou 2024: 31, 35.
[84] Cf. Fine 1993: 290n13. For the reliability of Aristotle as a witness to Plato, see Sections 3.5 and 5.2.
[85] There is an obvious difficulty here in appearing to side with Aristotle against Plato regarding what Plato himself said, given the presence of passages in Plato which seem to support the existence of Forms of artefacts (and it may actually be Xenocrates who excluded Forms of artefacts: see Sedley 2021: 34). Perhaps Plato chose to make such statements for the purposes of exposition. In the *Timaeus*, Plato presents a myth describing the temporal generation of the world, although many Platonists held that Plato himself did not posit such a generation, but was only using the myth to explain how the cosmos was ordered on rational lines.
[86] Politis 2020: 57. His reason is that by concentrating on the conception of philosophy (psychology with a political element) presented in the *Seventh Letter* – a concept shaped by its context – we would arrive at a different understanding of philosophy than that which Plato presents in the dialogues.
[87] Burnyeat 2015: 122.

is evidence of Plato's Unwritten Doctrines within works free from question marks concerning their authenticity (such as the *Republic*), this should not vitiate the Tübingen position. Furthermore, the *Seventh Letter* criticises writing in a manner consistent with the *Phaedrus*. Szlezák, in particular, has advanced cogent arguments for the existence of Plato's oral teaching independent of the *Seventh Letter* in a manner that could be accepted, even by those who doubt its authenticity.[88]

Why should Plato hesitate to make certain aspects of his thought public? One factor was certainly his own disastrous public lecture(s) on the Good.[89] The event was ridiculed on the Athenian comic stage even after Plato's death.[90] Such a setback must have triggered a subsequent reticence in revealing philosophical insights to those incapable of appreciating their value. This episode underscores how vital it is to be open to information contained in the testimonia and the extent to which they can elucidate the dialogues – a key aspect of the methodology employed by the Tübingen School.[91] Here we have evidence for Plato's teaching concerning the Theory of Principles, an example of something more valuable than the insights found in writing. (It might be argued that Plato's oral teaching was not spared from the sort of fate which he envisaged for writing: his lecture addressed itself to the wrong sort of audience, but it did at least not suffer from the other two deficiencies.)

In the *Seventh Letter*, which recounts Plato's attempt to educate Dionysius, the tyrant of Syracuse, in philosophical matters, the author's criticism of Dionysius is not primarily concerned with the revelation of esoteric knowledge (although Dionysius gave the Principles 'discordant and inappropriate publicity', *Epist.* VII 345d), but with making information public in written form which he himself did not even understand (with the reproach of plagiarism thrown in for good measure; cf. *Epist.* VII 345e).[92]

> This was what I said to Dionysius at that time. I did not explain everything to him nor did Dionysius ask, for he claimed to know many and even the most important doctrines – sufficiently well by means of the hearsay of others. And

---

[88] E.g. Szlezák 2019a: 323. Szlezák 2021: 612–615 also criticises the grounds for rejecting the authenticity of the *Seventh Letter*.
[89] Passage discussed and quoted in full at Section 1.3.
[90] Alexis fr. 152 (II 353 Kock); Amphis fr. 6 (II 237 Kock); Philippides fr. 6 (II 303 Kock). The references are to Plato's Good, rather than the lecture(s), but it is likely that Plato's Good became well known in Athens due to public teaching; see Gaiser 1980: 11–12.
[91] In other words, whether one agrees with the arguments advanced by the Tübingen School or not, the scholarship used to support these positions is methodologically sound.
[92] The author outlines more severe grievances against Dionysius at 335c–335e (including a family land dispute at 345c–345d), but these are less relevant to the matter at hand. Cf. Reale 2010: 87–88 on the need for the author to have knowledge.

I hear that later he wrote about what he heard then, framing it as his own skill and nothing of what he had heard. (*Epist.* VII 341a5–341b3)

Note that the criticism is levelled against revealing the principles in written form; the author has clearly not even read the book, as is clear from this passage (341b3–341b5).[93] The situation he finds himself in is similar to that of Zeno, whose book was stolen and who consequently lost the option of deciding whether to make his teachings public or not (*Parm.* 128d7–128e1): 'It was with such a love of contentiousness that I wrote it [Zeno's text] when young, and after it was written, someone stole it, so that I could not deliberate whether it should be brought to light or not.'[94] The author goes on to explain why there is no Platonic dialogue which clarifies the doctrine of the principles (although it is in the background or hinted at in several dialogues such as the *Parmenides*, the *Philebus*, and the *Timaeus*).[95]

> There does not exist – nor will there ever exist – any writing (*suggramma*) of mine about these matters. For it is not sayable like other studies, but from habitual association (with a teacher) and communion concerning the subject itself, suddenly just like a light inflamed by a leaping fire, it is brought to birth in the soul and nourishes itself. . . . And if it seemed to me that these matters should be sufficiently expressed in writing or verbally for the public, what could I have accomplished nobler than this, than to write something of such great use to humanity and to bring to light the nature of things for all. (*Epist.* VII 341c4–341e1)

The author highlights the deficiency of writing, rather than the necessity of keeping knowledge secret, advancing similar arguments to those of the *Phaedrus*, noting especially the arrogance of those who think that they can learn from written texts (*Epist.* VII 341e; cf. *Phdr.* 275a–275b). The only possible justification for writing such things down, as a mnemonic device (cf. *Phdr.* 275a), is discounted in this case since the insight of the principles would not be forgotten once grasped (*Epist.* VII 345d). A philosophical text, as stated before, will not contain the 'most valuable' things:

> On account of this, every earnest man dealing with serious subjects will avoid writing so that he might not lay them open to envy and misunderstanding among men. In a word, it may be known by this that when one sees written compositions, whether the laws of a lawgiver or any other thing in another form, these are not serious, if the author is serious, rather they are in his most beautiful region [i.e. they remain in his head]. However, if he has put earnest

---

[93] Szlezák 2004: 57–58.   [94] Szlezák 2004: 12.
[95] Strictly speaking, he mentions a 'true doctrine' here, but subsequently discloses that he is referring to principles, *Epist.* VII 345d–345e.

matters in writing, it is because 'mortal men, not the gods, have taken away his mind'. (*Epist.* VII 344c1–344d1)

2.4 The 'Deliberate Gaps' (*Aussparungsstellen*) and Their Purpose

Plato further indicated that his own dialogues are not exempt from the deficiencies which he identified with writing in the deliberate gaps: points where Plato hints that there is a solution to a particular question he poses, but which he chooses not to answer within the dialogue itself.[96] Indeed, the motif of concealment occurs regularly throughout the dialogues. For example, Socrates mentions 'the longer road' of philosophical examination at *Rep.* IV 435c–435d, notes at *Rep.* VI 506d2–507a2 that discovering the essence of the Good is more than can be achieved with 'our present onrush' and, at *Rep.* VI 509c, admits that he is leaving out many things in the analogy of the sun. Similarly, at *Rep.* VII 533a, Socrates confesses that Glaucon would not be able to follow the full account of dialectic. There are similar gaps in other dialogues which are explicitly thematised or hinted at. At *Plt.* 284d, the demonstration provided is simply adequate for the purposes of the present discussion (suggesting that there is a better sort of demonstration). At *Parm.* 136d–136e, Zeno comments that it is not suitable for Parmenides to speak on such subjects before the many, especially at his age, for the many do not know that, except by this devious passage through all things, the mind cannot attain to the truth. It is not just the philosophical expert (usually Socrates, but also Timaeus) who seeks to withhold his knowledge, but even the less sophisticated interlocutors: Euthydemus and Dionysodorus do the same in the *Euthydemus*, as do Euthyphro and Cratylus in the dialogues which bear their names.[97]

These deliberate gaps refer to both the Form (or Idea) of the Good and the structure of the soul. However, Socrates does have a solution and would be willing to carry the discussion further: 'for my part, enthusiasm would not be absent' (*Rep.* VII 533a2), were it not that his interlocutor (and the occasion) is unsuitable. While several of the dialogues contain deliberate gaps or hint at the Theory of Principles (or in the case of the *Parmenides* or the *Philebus* do more than merely hint), it is the *Republic* which plays a central role in this regard. Glaucon urges Socrates to discuss the Good, prompting the following response from Socrates (*Rep.* VI 506d7–507a2):

---

[96] Several of the texts highlighting these gaps are supplied at Krämer 1990: 199–202: *Prt.* 356e8–357c1; *Meno* 76e3–77b1; *Phd.* 107b4–1074b10; *Rep.* VI 506d2–507a2; *Rep.* VI 509c1–509c11; *Parm.* 136d4–136e3; *Soph.* 254b7–254d4; *Plt.* 284a1–284e4; *Tim.* 48c2–48e1; *Tim.* 54c4–54d7 with a further reference to the Unwritten Doctrines (but not a deliberate gap) at *Laws* X 894a1–894a5.

[97] Szlezák 1999: 9–10.

> But I fear that I shall not manage and that, in my ardent desire, I shall become a source of laughter. But, my excellent friends, let us leave alone for the present what precisely the Good is. For it seems to me that to reach what is in my mind at the moment is beyond the current onrush. But I am disposed to say what appears to be the offspring of the Good and most similar to it, if it pleases you, but if not, let it be.

Glaucon does not quite let Socrates off the hook, suggesting that he can elaborate on the Good at another time. This motif of attempting to compel Socrates to reveal more than he is prepared to say reoccurs throughout the *Republic*. It would be unreasonable to expect Plato to reveal more concerning the Idea of the Good when ascent to this principle constitutes the capstone of his educational programme in the ideal state of Kallipolis and will only be attainable by those who follow intensive philosophical study after the age of fifty (*Rep.* VII 540a).[98]

Plato's stress on the 'longer road' is significant and demands a clarification; there have been suggestions that it refers to something other than a deliberate gap. Sarah Broadie suggests that this 'longer road' may refer either to the soul (when interpreted at the point at which the reference is made) or the virtues as studied by the philosopher-rulers-in-training (when read from the perspective of VI 504a–504b).[99] For Broadie, the shorter road is travelled by Socrates' companions and the *Republic*'s readers, while the longer road is that of the philosopher-kings.[100] Similarly, Terry Penner suggests that the 'longer road' refers to a second account that will allow us to grasp Justice, Temperance, Courage, and Wisdom in the individual.[101]

Plato's reticence regarding the Good has also been commented on in the non-Tübingen tradition. Broadie highlights that 'direct words' would not be effective in explaining the Idea of the Good, either to Socrates' interlocutors or to the *Republic*'s readers; Plato instead prefers to sketch it by means of analogy (the sun) or with reference to the method which engages with it (dialectic).[102] Broadie, though, attributes this strategy to linguistic poverty, rather than to the existence of oral doctrines.[103] She also highlights Socrates' claim that Glaucon could not follow the discussion at 533a1–533a2, though with a different emphasis, linking it with Diotima's assertion at *Symp.* 210a2–210a4 (in terms reminiscent of the Mysteries) that Socrates will not be able to follow. The point of the passage, then, could be a rejection of the model of the Mysteries (rather than a deliberate gap).[104] Broadie suggests that if this were a reference to the oral doctrines one would expect some 'positive evidence' for

---

[98] Szlezák 1999: 10. [99] Broadie 2021: 3–4. [100] Broadie 2021: 48.
[101] Penner 2007a: 27. [102] Broadie 2021: 17. [103] Broadie 2021: 21.
[104] Broadie 2021: 104–105.

these doctrines (particularly the principles) and downplays the notion that glimpsing the Good can be regarded as exclusive.[105]

Although unwilling explicitly to treat the nature of the Good, in *Republic* Books VI and VII, Plato's Socrates does speak about it by means of images (the allegory of the cave and the analogy of the sun, while the analogy of the divided line describes the ascent to the Good, as does the allegory of the cave). *Republic* VI and VII can be regarded as containing particularly well-flagged deliberate gaps. The allegory of the cave (*Rep.* VII 514a–520a) is probably Plato's most famous passage. Prisoners chained up in a cave see only shadows of objects reflected on the cave wall. A prisoner manages to escape the cave and first sees shadows of objects on the ground outside the cave before being able to raise his eyes to the heavenly bodies 'and finally, I suppose, he would be able to see the sun, not images of it in water or some strange place, but the sun itself, in its own place, and be able to contemplate what it is' (*Rep.* VII 516b4–516b7). The sun represents the Idea of the Good, the heavenly bodies the value Forms, and the animals and plants outside the cave the mathematical Forms, while the shadows inside the cave represent images in the sense-perceptible world.[106]

As we know from the preceding analogy of the sun (*Rep.* VI 508b–509c), just as the sun is the source of vision in the sense-perceptible world, so too is the Good the source of understanding in the intelligible world (*Rep.* VI 508c). Glaucon's inability to comprehend the Good's nature (as well as the deficiency of writing to convey this insight to the reader who lacks this level of understanding) forces Socrates to speak in images. He highlights that he is omitting a great deal, noting in response to Glaucon's attempt to compel him to omit nothing: 'I think that I will have to leave a lot out, but, at present, as far as possible, I will not leave out anything willingly' (*Rep.* VI 509c9–509c10).

The analogy of the divided line (*Rep.* VI 509d–511e) envisages a line divided in two unequal parts, the shorter part of the line corresponding to the sense-perceptible world and the longer part to the intelligible realm. (Both of these subdivisions are in turn subdivided in two.) This analogy explains Plato's epistemology, as well as his metaphysics, although all of its details need not concern us here. Of immediate relevance is that the line traces increasing levels of reality from images of visible things (shadows and reflections) to visible things themselves and, in the upper subdivisions of the line, mathematical Forms and the higher Forms, culminating with the Idea of the Good itself. In the lower section of the divided line, by using images the soul proceeds to a conclusion, not a First Principle (*Rep.* VI 510b9) and it is only in the upper section of the line, by proceeding via the study of Forms, that the soul can arrive

---

[105] Broadie 2021: 106, 134. On the principles, Broadie 2021: 216.   [106] Sedley 2016: 22.

at a First Principle: 'Having attained this [the unhypothetical First Principle of all], it again takes hold of the things that depend upon it and, in this manner, it descends to a conclusion, not availing of any sense-perceptible object, but only of the Forms themselves, through Forms to Forms and concluding in Forms' (*Rep.* VI 511b7–511c2).[107]

It is striking, then, that all three accounts of the Good supplied in *Republic* VI and VII explain its nature by making use of images while the *Republic* itself (and Plato's corpus more broadly) highlights the deficiency of images: this has been misunderstood by Schleiermacheanism, which exploits the notion of an image in the sense of being a copy. From a Schleiermachean perspective, Plato's own dialogues are equivalent to oral discourse since they are images of it (and therefore not subject to the *Phaedrus*' criticism of writing). This ignores Plato's own negative understanding of 'image', which is particularly forcefully developed in the *Republic*, in the context of the deficiency of images for understanding the principles and with the gaps in the discussion of this aspect of philosophical teaching explicitly underscored.[108] Furthermore, *Republic* X highlights the deficiency of the image of the bed, inferior to both the bed itself and the Form of Bed. Plato could hardly have done more to highlight that he did not regard something being an image in a positive light.

A criticism that can easily be advanced against the dialogues is that Socrates appears to deal only with incompetent interlocutors – or at least interlocutors who fall far short of his philosophical ability. When capable interlocutors are present, there is no dialogue. For example, the main philosophical content of the *Timaeus* is delivered as a monologue by the eponymous character. This is because, as noted by Szlezák, a discussion between two accomplished philosophers would be a discussion about the principles – that is, about a topic, which, as Plato has explicitly flagged, he reserves for oral defence.[109] This is indicated by the *Timaeus*' very obvious deliberate gap: it is made explicit that the cosmological discussion shall only go as far as the elementary triangles, but no further: 'but the principles which are even more ultimate that these only God knows and, of men, the one who is dear to him' (*Tim.* 53d6–53d7). Timaeus previously explained why: 'We shall not elucidate now the principle of everything – or their principles or whatever term is fitting, for no other reason except it is difficult, following the present manner of description, to disclose our opinions' (Plato, *Tim.* 48c2–48c6).

This helps to explain the relationship between the two strands of the tradition: the dialogues and the Unwritten Doctrines. Far from being an attempt to circumvent the restrictions of a written text via the dialogue form, the

---

[107] For a discussion of the identification of the Good with the non-hypothetical principle, see Seel 2007: 184–185.
[108] Reale 2010: 91–92.   [109] Szlezák 1999: 80.

Timaeus (just like the *Phaedrus*) highlights that it falls foul of the deficiencies inherent in all writing. Plato's dialogues should not be thought of as oral, but as what they are – writings which mimic (to some extent) orality. Since Timaeus is addressing Socrates, he could theoretically expound the Theory of Principles (although Critias would hardly be capable of following), but Plato is conscious that the written text is inadequate for this level of philosophical communication and flags the deliberate gaps.

2.5 What Is the Purpose of the Dialogues?

An obvious question then arises: given Plato's reservations towards writing, reservations regularly expressed throughout the course of his career and therefore not confined to the early part of his intellectual development and subsequently overcome – as Schleiermacher claims – what was the point of writing philosophical texts? After all, while there is a clear notion of play in Plato and, while writing is clearly subordinated to oral teaching, Plato must have attached some valuable purpose to writing (given the extent of his corpus and the polished nature of his literary legacy). A related question concerns the intended readership of the dialogues. Szlezák suggests that the dialogues could have been targeted towards different groups of readers (e.g. laypeople, those with the appropriate training and Plato's own students) and that these groups do not have to be mutually exclusive.[110]

One possibility – drawing on the criticism of writing in the *Phaedrus* – is that the dialogues serve a hypomnematic function – that is, they serve as a reminder to those readers who already have obtained the insights offered by the Theory of Principles. This would appear to conflict with the comments at *Epist.* VII 344d5–344e2: 'He did not write them down as mnemonic aids, for there is no fear that anyone might forget this if the soul has once caught hold of it, for it is contained in the shortest possible formula.' At the same time, for readers at a less advanced stage of philosophy (or indeed readers outside the Academy itself), the dialogues could serve a protreptic function – that is, turning such readers towards the study of philosophy which, for them, could ultimately culminate in grasping the insights offered by Plato's oral teaching, even if, for the moment, the dialogues only offer them deficient images while emphasising their own deficiency. After all, many of the early dialogues (e.g. *Laches*) end in *aporia* (i.e. apparent philosophical impasse). Yet far from being pointless, such aporetic dialogues serve as an encouragement to turn to the study of philosophy and find a solution.

---

[110] Szlezák 1999: 20.

3 Plato's Theory of Principles and the Testimonia

3.1 What Were Plato's Unwritten Doctrines?

While it can be difficult to see how the dialogues and the Unwritten Doctrines interrelate, they comprise the twin strands of Plato's philosophical legacy. August Böckh suggested that the Unwritten Doctrines are both the crown of Plato's system and the key revealing what is outlined in the dialogues.[111] As demonstrated in the preceding section, Plato held doctrines which were recounted orally. The general absence of an explicit treatment of these in the dialogues is repeatedly flagged at those points in the dialogues where such an excursus would prove relevant. Such doctrines offer insights superior to those offered by written texts (including his own). The next question to pose is what these doctrines actually are. While Plato leaves some deliberate gaps in relation to his doctrine of the soul (e.g. *Rep.* VI 435c–435d), the core of the Unwritten Doctrines consists of Plato's Theory of Principles. It seems clear that there was a set of principles which served as the basis of philosophising in the Academy (otherwise it is difficult to make sense of what Plato's immediate successors, Speusippus and Xenocrates, were up to when they attempted to systematise Plato). However, even if the principles are generally not brought (directly) into the dialogues, there are frequent indications (especially in dialogues such as the *Republic*, *Parmenides*, *Philebus*, and *Timaeus*) that they are relevant to the matter under discussion (e.g. the Good or world generation), which is not particularly surprising given the extent to which they underpin Plato's metaphysics.[112]

The principles consist of the One (often identified with the Idea of the Good) which serves as the principle of Unity and the Indefinite Dyad (in the context of the Old Academy sometimes referred to as the Great and Small, μέγα καὶ μικρόν) which accounts for multiplicity. The entire history of metaphysics can be presented (as it was by the German Idealists and Halfwassen) as the attempt to explain how multiplicity is derived from unity so this Theory of Principles firmly locates Plato within a tradition stretching from the Presocratics to Hegel.[113]

There are other passages which lend themselves to being read in terms of the Theory of Principles (and certainly were read this way by, e.g. Proclus), such as the myth of Atlantis (*Tim.* 21e–25d; *Criti.* 108c–120d) with antediluvian Athens

---

[111] Böckh 1872: 5–9; qt. at Krämer 1990: 29; cf. Reale 1990: xviii.

[112] Opponents of the Tübingen School's approach deny that there are references to the principles, often by not identifying the Good of the *Republic* with the One. See Section 5 and O'Brien 2019: 18.

[113] Hegel [1832] 1986: 100 famously referred to philosophy as 'the study of the determination of unity'. Cf. O'Brien 2021a: xxii.

being taken to symbolise the One and Atlantis the Indefinite Dyad. However, since this requires a strongly allegorical reading which goes far beyond anything Plato says in the text of either the *Timaeus* or the *Critias*, it lies beyond the scope of our current discussion.[114]

The theory posits two opposed principles, although there are questions in interpreting the manner in which these principles interact with each other and to what extent the Indefinite Dyad can be regarded as a principle. The principles are not equal: the One is the First Principle and 'ontologically prior' to the Indefinite Dyad. In the attempt to get back to a first principle, the more simple entity is prior to the more complex one, since the more complex one can be broken up into its simpler components. To use a more tangible example, hydrogen and oxygen can be regarded as prior to water since water can be broken down into these more simple components.

Can the Theory of Principles be reconstructed? Yes (both from the indirect tradition and, in an abbreviated manner, from the dialogues), precisely because it was no great secret. The testimonia of Aristotle and the report of Sextus Empiricus supply us with ample information in this regard. Even when Plato indicates the inadequacy of treating his theory in written form, he still provides sufficient information for us to work out what this theory is.

3.2 The One and Indefinite Dyad

While the Theory of Principles posits principles of unity and multiplicity, the principles can be viewed in different terms: the One as a principle of determinacy and the Indefinite Dyad as a principle of indeterminacy. The One is identified with the Good since – as Gaiser suggests – unity is the basis of order, which allows it to be viewed as the basis of virtue.[115] Krämer's groundbreaking study analysed Plato's ontology from the perspective of virtue.[116] Even a dialogue such as the *Timaeus,* which describes the arrangement of the cosmos in terms of geometric and mathematical organisation, thematises the connection with the Good (and the Beautiful) since this arrangement is described as the best and the most beautiful.[117] The principles should not be conceived of as abstractions since they already contain everything; rather we should think of the theory in terms of a reduction of opposites to the One and Indefinite Dyad.[118] Everything results from the interaction of the two principles: exactly how was the subject of extensive speculation in the subsequent Platonic tradition. The One equalises while the Dyad renders into a multiplicity (either by dividing or halving).[119] The

---

[114] See O'Brien forthcoming.   [115] Gaiser 1968: 19.   [116] Krämer 1959.
[117] Gaiser 1968: 73.   [118] Gaiser 1968: 18–19, 80.
[119] Aristotle, *Met.* 1081a–1081b; *Phlb.* 25d–25e; Gaiser 1968: 117, 541.

effect of the equalising First Principle is clear when, for example, in the act of halving, both halves are of equal size.[120] The theory is brilliant in its (apparent) simplicity. Aristotle provides a succinct summary:

> Plato determined this concerning the subject of this investigation. It is obvious from what has been said that he employed only two principles, one of essence and the other of matter (for the Forms are the essential causes of the other things and the One the cause of the Forms) and he says what the underlying material is of which the Forms are predicated in the case of the sensible things and the One in the case of the Forms, it is the Dyad, the Great and the Small and, furthermore, he attributed causality for Good and for evil to each of the two principles. (*Met.* 988a7–988a15)

The claim that the Indefinite Dyad is the cause of evil seems like an unduly harsh formulation: it is certainly responsible for disorder, indicated by Necessity's role as an errant cause (but not a cause of evil) in the *Timaeus*. Simplicius presents the Indefinite Dyad as matter, rather than the cause of evil:

> For Plato held in his lectures *On the Good* that matter is the Great and Small, and he said that this is the Unlimited also and that all sense-perceptible things are encompassed by the Unlimited and are unknowable since their nature is in matter, unlimited and in a state of flux and Aristotle says that it appears to follow in this account that the Great and Small there, the very thing which is the Indefinite Dyad, is among the intelligibles and is itself a principle, together with the One of all number and of all beings. For the Forms are numbers too. (Simplicius, *In Phys.* 503, 12–18)

It is not due to a disinterest in fixed terminology that the One is identified with (the Idea of) the Good. As mentioned in Section 2, numbers are Forms, and while it is typical for scholars to distinguish between Form-Numbers and value Forms,[121] there is evidence to suggest that Plato was open to identifying non-number Forms with numbers, in this case, identifying the Good with the One (although there is a clear distinction between the One as a principle of unity and the number one). The notion is less surprising when we remember that the Pythagoreans regarded numbers as the principles and elements of everything.[122]

What is the philosophical value of Aristotle's presentation of the Unwritten Doctrines? If we regard Aristotle's report as being more valuable than mere polemic, then the question arises: what do the Form-Numbers actually explain? First, why does Plato posit Form-Numbers? Daniel Sung-hyun Yang argues that Form-Numbers account for the unity, structure, and order of numbers.[123] By contrast, Aristotle rejects Form-Numbers for a range of reasons (e.g. his attempt

---

[120] Gaiser 1968: 121. [121] Sedley 2016: 15.
[122] Sextus Empiricus, *Adv. Math.* X 248–283; Gaiser 1968: 82.
[123] Sung-hyun Yang 2024: 229.

to separate metaphysics and mathematics[124] and his objection to the relationship between Form-Number and the Platonist account of Being, illustrated by his opposition to Speusippus' approach).[125] Even if we reject Aristotle's critique, his report still raises important issues. For example, the Platonist account of number is generative – indicated by the One delimiting the Great and Small or touching other ones[126] – but this suggests, as does Aristotle's characterisation, that number is 'contiguous' while the notion of number as Forms requires that they are 'discrete'.[127] By concentrating on the problems that Aristotle is attempting to resolve with his own account of number, Sung-hyun Yang's analysis has demonstrated that (as far as this topic is concerned) Aristotle's report transcends polemic and that there are good grounds for treating Aristotle as a more valuable witness than he is generally given credit for. In my view, this applies also to his account of the principles. Furthermore, although a more detailed analysis of Form-Number beyond its connection with the Theory of Principles is beyond the scope of this Element, Speusippus'[128] (see Section 4.2) and Aristotle's speculations on this matter indicate that it clearly was a subject of intense discussion at the Academy;[129] this in turn reveals the Academy as an institution which encouraged open-ended enquiry rather than dogmatism.

How do Plato's principles explain the manner in which generation occurs? It cannot take place with both principles remaining static. An obvious suggestion is that generation would echo Empedocles' system of the alternating dominance of Love and Strife. Gaiser reads such a system into the *Statesman* myth (269c–274e) of the alternating ages of Cronos and of Zeus, in which Cronos first guides the world's revolutions in one direction, corresponding to a golden age and then, once Cronos has withdrawn to his conning tower during the age of Zeus, it revolves under its own power in the opposite direction. For Gaiser, these alternating ages represent the interplay of opposing principles, such as Same and Different.[130]

Although the *Timaeus* is explicitly not a dialogue on the principles, Szlezák reads them into the demiurgic myth since the *Timaeus* describes the construction of the world and it is necessary to mention the guiding principles to render this construction understandable.[131] The notion of principles is raised: 'Now everything that comes to be comes about of necessity, as we say, by means of some cause' (*Tim.* 28c2–28c3), for it would not be possible for anything to come to be without a cause, but Timaeus asserts that we shall not proceed to 'the

---

[124] Sung-hyun Yang 2024: 230; cf. *Met.* 1080a14–1080a36. [125] Sung-hyun Yang 2024: 237.
[126] *Parm.* 148d5–149d7. [127] Sung-hyun Yang 2024: 235.
[128] I.e. his principle of numbers and his rejection of Form-Numbers; cf. Aristotle's criticism of him at *Met.* 1028b21–1028b24.
[129] See *Met.* 1080a14–1080a36 for discussion on mathematical and ideal number.
[130] Gaiser 1968: 211. [131] Cf. Szlezák 2019a: 591.

principle of all things' – that is, what is prior to the elementary triangles (*Tim.* 48c2–48c6), themselves described as the 'principles of elementary bodies'.[132] (A similar topos is exhibited at *Cra.* 396a–396c, when Socrates, in the course of investigating the etymologies of divine names, claims that he is unable to ascend beyond the name of Cronos).[133]

The world results from the interaction between two forces or agents, described in two different ways in the *Timaeus*: as the Demiurge's ordering of the Receptacle or as the result of a compromise between Reason and Necessity. Since Reason is responsible for imposing determinacy and Necessity for Indeterminacy, they can be broadly viewed as representing the effects of the One and Indefinite Dyad, although since Reason corresponds to the demiurgic *nous*, or mind of the Craftsman-god, it cannot simply be equated with the One; we cannot ignore Timaeus' warning to those who fail to distinguish between the auxiliary causes and the causes (*Tim.* 46c–46e). Timaeus' stated reason for not discussing the principles – that they lie beyond the limits of human knowledge – is not particularly convincing: he subsequently (*Tim.* 53d6–53d7) notes that they are known to the man who is dear to the god (i.e. the philosopher), although they shall not be depicted here (i.e. this is another deliberate gap).[134] The *Timaeus* also highlights the nature of philosophical reticence: 'Now to find the maker and father of everything is a great task and, having found him, to narrate him *to everyone* is impossible' (*Tim.* 28c3–28c5).

Similarly, when he is about to embark on discussing the products of Necessity, Timaeus observes: 'the principle or principles of all things, or however I view them, should not be spoken of for the present on no other grounds other than it is difficult to illustrate my opinion *in accordance with the current method of exposition*' (*Tim.* 48c2–48c6) (my emphasis). If this is regarded as esotericism, it is plainly very different to the sort of esotericism which is generally attributed to the Tübingen School by their opponents. As Szlezák stresses, it is not that knowledge of the Demiurge cannot be conveyed, just that it cannot be conveyed 'to everyone' and it is not that Timaeus cannot talk about the principles; he can, just not 'for the present'.[135]

3.3 The Theory of Principles in the *Philebus*

The *Philebus*, one of Plato's last works, has long been regarded as a dialogue concerned with the Theory of Principles (as is the second part of the

---

[132] Szlezák 1999: 49.   [133] O'Brien 2019: 16.
[134] Szlezák 1999: 49; O'Brien 2021b: 94–95; see Section 2.4.
[135] Szlezák 2019a: 594. It might be argued that Timaeus is not talking about the One and Indefinite Dyad here, but lower 'principles'. The point is still relevant since if there are concerns about the discussion of lower causes, then surely these concerns are even more relevant in the case of higher ones.

Parmenides); Porphyry claimed that the *Philebus* actually outlined the teachings from Plato's lecture(s) on the Good.[136] (Although Schleiermacheans treat Plato's teaching on the Good as a single lecture, it does seem that he lectured on this topic on more than one occasion: Simplicius uses the plural 'logoi', *In Phys.* 453.28). Kevin Corrigan suggests that the *Philebus* comes closest to 'eavesdropping' on the conversations of the Old Academy, and it certainly marks a return to many of the *Republic*'s themes.[137] The ostensible topic of the discussion concerns whether the better aim of human life is knowledge or pleasure, although Socrates merely claims the superiority of knowledge over pleasure, rather than its status as the Good, before pivoting to the assertion that neither of them is a simple unity.[138] This opens the door to a metaphysical discussion, as Socrates initially outlines it: 'whatever is always said to be is from one and many, innately possessing Limit and the Unlimited' (*Phlb.* 16c9–16c10). So the discussion moves to consider the first principles of reality, although using in this context the Pythagorean terms of Limit (πέρας/Peras) and the Unlimited (ἄπειρον/Apeiron), rather than One and Indefinite Dyad. The mixture (of Peras and Apeiron) and the cause of this mixture (*nous* or mind) form part of this metaphysical scaffolding. From an historical perspective, Plato is influenced by Pythagorean dualism (since they posited the principles of Limit and Unlimited), and Eleatic monism, although where Parmenides and Zeno equate the One with Being and the Many with Non-Being, Plato places the One in opposition to Being (second hypothesis of the *Parmenides*, 142b–157b) and even beyond Being.[139]

Attention is also paid to the dialectical method, presented here as the processes of collection and division which enable greater understanding of these principles. It is only dialectic (i.e. the process that is depicted in the dialogues, but not the process of reading these dialogues) that permits knowledge of these principles.[140] The significance of dialectic is highlighted when Socrates – with a certain degree of literary licence, it must be admitted – equates dialectic, as the gift of the gods, with Prometheus' theft of fire from heaven. Gaiser highlights how Plato in the *Philebus* presents dialectic – and the ability to grasp the principles which it offers – as a key feature of the historical development of culture.[141]

The context here is significant since Socrates is actually discussing human language at this point and the unlimited number of tokens for types of vocal sound

---

[136] According to the testimony of Simplicius; cf. Sayre 2005: xiii.   [137] Corrigan 2023: 6.
[138] Ionescu 2019: 14.
[139] For an overview of the historical background, see Nikulin 2012a: 15. For Plotinus, the One is beyond even the opposition between Being and Non-Being.
[140] Ostenfeld 2010: 307.   [141] Gaiser 1968: 225.

(*Phlb*. 17b). However, since language is adopted as an analogy for the metaphysical discussion and, given that Plato in both the *Cratylus* and *Theaetetus* develops correspondences between linguistic structure and ontology, it is clear that this statement has further-reaching implications.[142] Corrigan – correctly in my view – regards Limit and Unlimited as 'the principles of everything' in the manner suggested in the Unwritten Doctrines:[143] Forms and 'those things which are most cognate to them (e.g. mathematicals). All other things must be designated secondary and later' (*Phlb*. 59c4–59c6). In spite of the differences in terminology, it is clear that the *Philebus* outlines a Theory of Principles similar to that indicated in the testimonia concerning the Unwritten Doctrines: a principle of unity/definition/determinacy and a principle of multiplicity/unboundedness/indeterminacy. Aristotle clarifies (*Met*. 987b26) that the Unlimited equates with the Dyad and the Great and Small (a term which suggests excess and deficiency).[144] Limit and the Unlimited are sometimes viewed as precursors to Aristotle's Form and matter:[145]

> Therefore, the Great and Small are principles as matter, just as the One is essence (*ousia*), for the numbers through participation in the One are derived from the Great and Small. However, by positing the One as a substance and not a predicate of some other thing, he is like the Pythagoreans and, in stating that the numbers are the causes of Being in the other things, he agrees with them. But he is unique in positing a Dyad, instead of an Unlimited that is single, and in making the Unlimited out of the Great and Small. (Aristotle, *Met*. 987b20–987b27)

Apeiron/Unlimited is characterised as multiplicity (*Phlb*. 24a2–25a4) and by lack of limit – for example, heat can always be 'more' or 'less'; there is no terminus – while Peras/Limit is more strictly delineated. Peras is opposed to disorder, while Apeiron lacks order.[146] If Apeiron is matter without Form, Aristotle claims, then it is unknowable (*Physics* 207a25–207a26), and if the Receptacle of Plato's *Timaeus* is regarded as equivalent to matter, then this would conflict with Plato's assertion that the Receptacle is 'graspable by some type of bastard calculation' (*Tim*. 52b2).[147]

As to the knowability of the First Principle, the One's unity is manifested by measure, beauty and truth:[148]

> Surely then if we cannot catch the Good with one idea, let us take hold of it with three – with beauty, with due proportion and with truth, and let us say that this, taken as if it were one, we may more correctly claim as the cause

---

[142] Gaiser 1968: 166.   [143] Corrigan 2023: 171.
[144] Sayre 2005: xvi; cf. Aristotle, *Physics* 187a16–187a20; Cherniss 1944: 84.
[145] Cf. Gaiser 1968: 313.   [146] See Gosling 1975: 187.
[147] Cherniss 1944: 111 suggests that Aristotle might have regarded this as a criticism of Plato.
[148] See Corrigan 2023: 166.

than anything else in the mixture and that, on account of this, the mixture itself has been rendered good. (*Phlb.* 65a1–65a5)[149]

Measure, beauty, and truth are Forms by means of which we can come to know the Good[150] by unifying this triad in the soul, stressing again the identification of the Good with the One.[151] This echoes the relationship between the Beautiful and the Good in the *Symposium*, where Beauty is a high-level Form which serves as an intermediary to knowledge of the Good, but yet is distinguished from the Good.

Even if the Beautiful occupies the highest point in Diotima's ladder of ascent in the *Symposium* and the ascent depicted represents an ascent to the Good, symbolised by the *Symposium*'s movement to the house of Agathon (wordplay on the Greek for good), the Good and the Beautiful are not synonymous;[152] the Beautiful occupies its position in Diotima's ladder since it facilitates the ascent to the Good. The *Symposium*, though, distinguishes between the Beautiful and the Good (e.g. at *Symp.* 172b, 201b), yet it is also clear – despite the representation of the Beautiful as the aim of the soul's ascent – that the Beautiful is subordinated to the Good, just as at *Rep.* 508e (quoted in Section 3.4). Throughout the dialogue, Plato represents the Beautiful as an object of desire, but it is the Good which makes this visible and intelligible (*Symp.* 211d–212a).[153] This connection between the Beautiful and the Good is echoed in the *Philebus*:

> Socrates: Now the power of the Good has sought refuge in the nature of the Beautiful. For moderation and due proportion are everywhere a characteristic of beauty and virtue, no doubt. (*Phlb.* 64e5–64e7)

Similarly, while Aristotle identifies the Unlimited/Apeiron with the Indefinite Dyad, it is more difficult to advance the case that Limit/Peras should be identified with the One. Although Findlay notes that Plato does not identify Limit with the One, he suggests that it is 'plainly a variant';[154] Aristotle (*Met.* 987a15–a19) also identifies Limit with the One (although there he moves between referring to the Pythagoreans and Plato). Yet Plato at 16c9–16c10 does not identify the One with Limit; he claims the One and Many as principles and notes that all things have Limit and Unlimited within them. Limit is not the

---

[149] Seel 2007: 192 uses this passage to argue that the Good cannot be conceived of as a single Form, but rather as a combination of several Forms; this highlights the difference of the Good in comparison with (other) Forms, but devalues the radical transcendence which the Tübingen School stresses.
[150] Corrigan 2023: 186.   [151] Gerson 2023: 179.
[152] In fact, they are repeatedly distinguished in the *Symposium*: e.g. 201b and, more significantly, at 205e–207a. See Corrigan 2023: 146–148.
[153] Corrigan 2023: 147.   [154] Findlay 1974: 280.

One since it becomes good to the extent to which it is imposed by its cause (*nous*).[155]

Let us return to Socrates' distinction between four kinds: Unlimited, Limit, mixture, and cause:

> Accordingly, I count the Unlimited first, Limit second, then as third the Being (*ousia*) mixed and produced out of these. And if I count as four the cause (*aitia*) of this mixture and production, would I not strike a false note? (*Phlb.* 27b7–27c1)

Yet at *Phlb.* 23d–23e, Protarchus asks whether there is a need for a fifth kind with 'the capacity of separation' to which Socrates assents, although noting 'not at the moment'. I would follow Corrigan's reading here that this fifth kind is the Good – explicitly marked off from the other kinds, as we have been told that the Good should be.[156] In fact, Socrates' explicit decision not to investigate the fifth kind at this point – while still alluding to it – can be regarded as a deliberate gap.

3.4 The Theory of Principles and the Theory of Forms

There are good reasons for regarding the Theory of Principles, rather than the Theory of Forms, as the most characteristic of Plato's doctrines (see Section 1), but, in any case, the Forms depend upon the principles, so the two theories are interrelated, rather than mutually exclusive.[157] Dialectic is valuable since it permits knowledge of both the Forms and the principles: 'and may we not also claim that only the power of dialectic may reveal this to the one experienced in what we have recounted, but it is not possible by any other means?' (*Rep.* VII 533a8–533a10). That the Theory of Forms can be subsumed into the Theory of Principles supports the claim that the Theory of Principles is a more fundamental doctrine of Plato's: the principles are even more basic than the Forms which depend upon them.

Other reasons supporting this viewpoint are:

1. While the Theory of Forms resolves various metaphysical and epistemological matters, the Theory of Principles explains a more fundamental metaphysical concern: the derivation of multiplicity from unity.
2. It can be claimed that Plato rejects the Theory of Forms (or at least criticises it heavily) in the *Parmenides*, although the *Timaeus* (a late dialogue) presupposes the existence of the Forms.

---

[155] Gerson 2023: 178. This corresponds to the goodness of the cosmos which becomes good to the extent that it is ordered in accordance with the Forms by the demiurgic *nous* in the *Timaeus*.

[156] Corrigan 2023: 188.

[157] In Middle Platonist interpretations (i.e. from Antiochus of Ascalon until the development of Neoplatonism under Plotinus), the Forms cease to be separate principles but are regarded as the thoughts of God. Cf. O'Brien 2015: 48.

Since both theories are interrelated, it is not my primary aim to argue for the greater significance of the Theory of Principles; rather I wish to underscore that the Theory of Principles is not a doctrine of Plato's dotage (as it is sometimes misrepresented) and should not therefore be regarded as an aberration of his thought, but as central to his entire philosophical project.[158]

According to the testimony of Aristotle, *Met.* 1091b13–1091b15, the Good is regularly identified with the One: 'Of those who claim that there are unchangeable essences, some assert that the One itself is the Good itself, however, they supposed that its essence consisted chiefly of oneness/unity.' Generally (and, to my mind, regrettably), there is a strong tendency to present the Good as simply another Form, rather than to stress its radical transcendence and difference in nature from everything which it transcends, as highlighted by Halfwassen and Gerson.[159] Similarly, Dirk Baltzly argues that the approach to the Good differs from knowledge of the other Forms.[160] Plato certainly refers to the Good as a Form or Idea (ἰδέα, *Rep.* VI 505a, 508a, 508e; VII 517b, 534b) and as a paradigm (παράδειγμα, *Rep.* VII 540a).[161] Those presenting the Good as just another Form sometimes point to a certain claimed ambiguity at, for example, *Rep.* VI 507b4–507b6.[162]

Yet it is clear that the Good is distinguished from the other Forms since it is their cause: 'it is in a certain sense the cause of all these things' (*Rep.* VII 516c1–516c2). Furthermore, other Forms are merely boniform (ἀγαθοειδή; *Rep.* 508e5–509a5) and distinguished from the Good itself (*Rep.* VI 509a). It is the Good which makes the Forms knowable:

> Accordingly, *assert that what gives truth to the objects of knowledge and the power [of knowledge] to the knower is the Idea of the Good* and you must consider it the cause of knowledge and of truth so far as is known. Although they are both beautiful, knowledge and truth, *in believing it to be something other than and even more beautiful than these, you will think correctly*. (*Rep.* VI 508e1–508e6; my italics)

The special status of the Good (i.e. marked out from the other Forms) is made explicit, even when Plato refers to it as a Form, illustrated, for example, by the manner in which the Good surpasses even a high-level Form such as the Beautiful. The Good is the basis for knowledge (cf. *Rep.* VII 540a) and at

---

[158] Schleiermacher placed the *Republic* in Plato's late – rather than middle – period, marginalising the significance of the deliberate gaps there; cf. O'Brien 2019: 91–92.

[159] E.g. Halfwassen 2015: 22 and Gerson 2023: 30. See O'Brien 2019.

[160] Baltzly 1996: 158–159.

[161] O'Brien 2019: 31. Some scholars (e.g. Ferber and Damschen 2015; cf. the treatment at Corrigan 2023: 151–152) deny that the Good can even be an Idea at all.

[162] Gerson 2020: 164n6: The passage permits an argument that the Good is not actually 'beyond Being'.

Rep. VI 505d11–505e1 is regarded as the basis for all human motivation: 'And every soul pursues the Good and does everything that it does because of it.' Plato stresses that it stands apart:

> In the realm of the known, the Idea of the Good is the last thing to be seen and seen with difficulty. But, when seen, one must infer that it is the cause of everything correct and beautiful in all things, that in the visible realm it gives birth to light and its source and, in the intelligible world, it furnishes authentic truth and reason, so that it is necessary for anyone who is to act rationally in private or public to see it. (*Rep.* VII 517b7–517c5)

Furthermore, Socrates explicitly notes that 'the nature of the Good differs from other things' (*Phlb.* 60b10).

It seems that Plato went beyond regarding the Forms simply as causes of other things (as in the *Phaedo*), viewing them as caused, in turn, by the principles. The *Philebus*, for example, makes explicit the dependence of the Forms upon higher principles (*Phlb.* 61d1–61e1),[163] reflected by Aristotle's remark at *Met.* 987b18–987c22 that Unity and the Great and the Small (i.e. the One and Indefinite Dyad) are the elements of the Forms and that the numbers are generated from the Great and Small's interaction with Unity. Aristotle claims here that Plato regarded the numbers as the causes of other things, a role elsewhere attributed to the Forms, but since Plato regarded numbers as Forms (or, strictly speaking, as a certain type of Form), there would not seem to be any concerning discrepancy here.[164] Sensible things come about as a result of the Forms and the Great and Small. Even at *Phaedo* 99b–99c, Socrates highlights that those who misidentify the auxiliary causes with the primary ones (i.e. the principles) are 'groping in the dark' (99b4–99b5) and 'truly they pay no thought to the Good which must connect and cohere all things' (99c5–99c6).

Those who try to downplay the Good's radical transcendence cling to the claim that it is still in the knowable realm (*Rep.* VI 517b), but this radical transcendence seems to be clear from the following passage:

> In a similar way [as the sun] say that from the presence of the Good, the objects of knowledge receive not only being known, but also existence and Being (*ousia*) belong to them from it, but [the Good] *is not Being* but is even *beyond Being* in dignity and transcending power. (*Rep.* VI 509b6–509b10; my italics)

---

[163] The passage deals with a kind of science truer than that which deals with what comes to be and perishes and instead deals with what is eternal.

[164] Numbers in Plato can denote measures (which includes arithmetical numbers), associated in the *Philebus* not just with music and heat, but also beauty, strength, and health (*Phlb.* 26b); such measures can be regarded as Forms. Cf. Sayre 2005: 115.

While adherents of the Tübingen School would read this as a clear reference to the First Principle, there are those who would deny the Good's identification with the One. There is a great deal at stake with this identification since if we accept it (and argue for the Good's radical transcendence), the Theory of Principles is clearly at the heart of one of Plato's key works. There are, however, other passages which can be marshalled in support of the claim that the Good belongs to the realm of Being: Plato refers to the Good as 'the brightest part of Being' (*Rep.* VII 518c9) and 'the most blessed aspect of Being' (*Rep.* VII 526e3–526e4).[165]

Other arguments beyond textual ones can also be employed: the Good belongs to the intelligible realm, just as the sun, which serves as an analogy for it, belongs to the visible one. Yet the assertion that 'in the region of the known the last thing to be seen and seen with difficulty is the Idea of the Good' (*Rep.* VII 517b8–c1) and Socrates' claim that it is 'beyond Being' both emphasise its distinction from the other entities presented as Forms. Furthermore, Aristotle's identification of the Good with the One (*Met.* 1091b13–1091b15),[166] the correspondences between the Good and the One of *Parmenides* 141e–142a and the Good's role as the cause of everything clearly positions it as the First Principle.[167]

3.5 Evaluating the Testimonia

The Unwritten Doctrines present us with a dilemma: if no traces of them can be found in the dialogues (which is sometimes claimed, but which I would dispute), then we are either compelled to study Aristotle for the highest insights of Plato's philosophy or we are forced to discount Aristotle's testimony altogether (see Section 5.2).[168]

If evidence of the Unwritten Doctrines can be ascertained independently of Aristotle (and preferably from the works of Plato himself), then such concerns become moot. The reality is that some dialogues do allude (in a much less explicit form) to the doctrines that are outlined more forcefully in the testimonia – or as Sayre notes (referring to the *Philebus*) – with different terminology.[169] Plato himself does not use the terms 'Great and Small' or 'Indefinite Dyad' in the dialogues, but employs the 'Unlimited' (used to refer to the Indefinite Dyad by Aristotle and Simplicius) and 'Unlimited Nature' (used also by Simplicius) in the *Philebus* to denote something similar.[170] Sayre's remark that 'Aristotle had neither the audacity nor the incentive completely to falsify the views he heard

---

[165] O'Brien 2019: 31; Corrigan 2023: 151.
[166] I have already advanced arguments for why we can accept the testimony of Aristotle.
[167] Corrigan 2023: 162.   [168] Sayre 2005: 11, 78.   [169] Sayre 2005: 13.
[170] Sayre 2005: 95.

Plato expounding' appears to be confirmed by references to the principles within the dialogues.[171] I leave aside the thorny question of at what point in his career Plato had formulated the Theory of Principles; it certainly is present in the *Republic* from his middle period. The contents of Plato's lecture(s) on the Good, then, are reflected in the *Republic*, *Symposium* and the *Philebus*.

3.6 The Dialogues and the Testimonia

Gaiser suggests two significant ways in which the dialogues relate to the oral teachings: first, via their protreptic orientation and, second, via the pedagogical imitation conveyed in the dialogues.[172] For Corrigan, the dialogues 'necessarily imply' the Unwritten Doctrines.[173] Even if we can reconstruct the Unwritten Doctrines from the dialogues, are we still left with the same version of the Theory of Principles as found in the testimonia? There appear to be some divergences: Socrates only speaks of one principle – the Good – in the *Republic*. Although there are claims (e.g. by Wolfgang Kullmann)[174] that the dialogues are monist while the testimonia are dualist, this is inaccurate; it does not conform with the readings of the *Philebus* and *Timaeus* presented here.[175] Nikulin observes that positing two principles is Hegelian and one principle is Plotinian.[176]

Halfwassen offers the most elegant solution (and also the most historically accurate, since it conforms most closely to what has been attested as far back as Speusippus): 'reductive monism and deductive dualism' (i.e. the Indefinite Dyad is not coequal with the One which is the basis of all reality, the Absolute, while two principles are required to account for the derivation of all things, although the Indefinite Dyad is not in any sense an absolute, even if it must be presupposed in any derivation from the One).[177] As Halfwassen has demonstrated, this conforms with the dualism found in the testimonia, as well as the *Philebus*, which in spite of the two principles it presents, Limit and Unlimited, still stresses a 'final monism'.[178] This is apparent from the *Philebus*' claims that each principle is one (23e, although Plato also attributes multiplicity to Peras) and that the Unlimited, despite its multiplicity, at least preserves the appearance of unity (26c–26d). Since the principle of multiplicity – as Halfwassen notes – must have an element of unity (otherwise it would not be anything at all), then this necessarily means that it is subordinate to the

---

[171] Sayre 2005: 83.   [172] Gaiser 1968: 6.   [173] Corrigan 2023: 7.
[174] Kullmann 1991: 11–21.
[175] Nor with the *Sophist* or *Parmenides*; cf. Halfwassen 2012: 144.   [176] Nikulin 2012a: 20.
[177] Halfwassen 2012: 149. Nikulin 2012a: 30–36 outlines how *reduction to the principles* and *deduction from the principles* functions.
[178] Halfwassen 2012: 147–150.

One as the ground of all unity. The testimonia do not actually contain an account of how the Indefinite Dyad is derived from the One, although Sextus Empiricus' report (*Adv. Math.* X 261 = *TP* 32 Gaiser) mentions the self-division of the One leading to the Indefinite Dyad. Halfwassen finds this account unsatisfactory, since Sextus presupposes otherness in the One as the basis of this self-division, when the One should be beyond otherness;[179] he confirms the historical accuracy of his solution via a passage from Speusippus (discussed at Section 4.2).[180] This preeminence of the principle of unity, then, actually corresponds with what we find in the testimonia (despite some claims to the contrary).

4 Consequences of the Tübingen School Approach for Later Platonism

4.1 The Principles and Developments within Platonism

The purpose of this section is to examine the consequences of accepting that Plato posited a Theory of Principles for our understanding of the development of the Platonic tradition and the history of philosophy more broadly. There are advantages to positing such a theory since, without it, it becomes difficult to make sense of the attempts to systematise Plato within the Old Academy, especially the work of Speusippus and Xenocrates. Naturally, this does not mean that we have to accept the existence of the Theory of Principles, but if we reject it, we need an alternative explanation for developments in the Academy. This explains why scholars influenced by the Tübingen School tend to downplay Neoplatonism as representing a break with Platonism and emphasise its continuity. To quote Halfwassen, the Tübingen School 'regards the philosophy of principles not as the latest phase of Plato's thought, but rather as the basis for the totality of his thought in all phases of its development'.[181]

4.2 The Old Academy

Consideration of developments in the Old Academy – mainly the systematisation of Plato's thought among his immediate successors – appears necessary due to the significance of the Theory of Principles for understanding subsequent Platonism. Numerous arguments can be advanced concerning the continuity of evidence for the oral tradition in the later Academy and (potentially) on into Neoplatonism, although this is hotly debated. Halfwassen (2015: 188, 215) argues for the continuity of the oral tradition within the Academy, exhibited, for example, by

---

[179] Cf. Halfwassen 1992: 282–286.
[180] Speusippus in Proclus, *In Parm.* VII 40, 1–5 Klibansky-Labowsky; fr. 62 Isnardi Parente = *TP* 50 Gaiser.
[181] Halfwassen 2021: 9.

Neopythagorean interpretations of the *Parmenides*, especially those of Eudorus and Moderatus.[182] Many sources on the Unwritten Doctrines represent the principles as Pythagorean (rather than Platonic);[183] this can be regarded as a 'backdating' conducted both within the Old Academy and by Iamblichus.[184] John Dillon suggests that the oral transmission of the Unwritten Doctrines broke down during the Sceptical Academy once Arcesilaus became scholarch in the mid 270s.[185] Even if we find it difficult to imagine that oral transmission could have survived these challenging circumstances, Plotinus clearly had access to Speusippus' interpretation of Plato's Theory of Principles; this is also documented by Proclus.

Cherniss advanced two arguments against this: the claim that no teaching took place at Plato's Academy (see Section 5.4)[186] and the assertion (based on Aristotle) that Speusippus, Plato's nephew and immediate successor as scholarch (head of the Academy) rejected the Theory of Forms.[187] Since this indicates that 'orthodoxy' was not required in the Academy, it can be used to cast doubt on arguments based on subsequent developments in the Academy as to the nature of Plato's thought.[188]

The Theory of Principles is so significant since the diverging responses to this theory divide Middle Platonism from Neoplatonism. While the Middle Platonists followed Xenocrates' (Speusippus' successor as scholarch) identification of the First Principle with Intellect, Plotinus reads Plato in the tradition of Speusippus, stressing the One's radical transcendence (i.e. beyond both Being and Intellect).[189] This is not to claim that the Theory of Principles is completely absent from Middle Platonism nor an attempt to present Xenocrates as unorthodox.[190] Rather, Xenocrates chose to emphasise and develop other aspects of Plato's thought, particularly a theology based upon Intellect and mediated by the *Timaeus*, which became highly influential in Middle Platonism. While many Middle Platonists were content to identify the First Principle with Being and Intellect, Plotinus correctly saw this as dragging the One down into multiplicity.[191] This is consistent with Plato's original concept of the First Principle. Even if we follow the Schleiermachean tradition and

---

[182] Halfwassen 2015: 188 argues that there is nothing specifically Pythagorean about a One beyond Being, which actually corresponds with inner-Academic doctrine. Also Halfwassen 2001: 47–65.

[183] On this, see Szlezák's (1999: 603) concept of camouflage, discussed at Section 5.4.

[184] Halfwassen 2021: 214.   [185] Dillon 2003: 16–17.   [186] Cherniss 1944: 165 and 1945: 72.

[187] Cherniss 1945: 38–39.

[188] Neither Speusippus or Xenocrates were 'orthodox', although see my treatment later in this section, while Plato himself engaged critically with the preceding Greek tradition (Frede 2018: 85, 99).

[189] Halfwassen 2015: 220–221; Cf. Dillon 2003: 107–108.

[190] We find it in Numenius. Cf. Halfwassen 2021: 215. On the influence of the *Timaeus* in Middle Platonism, see O'Brien 2015: 36–168.

[191] Halfwassen 2021: 216.

downplay the significance of the principles for *Plato* the philosopher, we cannot escape their importance for *Platonism*, the philosophical school.[192] Even Middle Platonism reveals the traces of the Theory of Principles since it too regards the First Principle as the basis of unity.

Cherniss' claim that Speusippus rejected the Theory of Forms is taken over wholesale from Aristotle, whose testimony he nevertheless simply dismisses when it supplies evidence supporting the Tübingen School. I would argue that Aristotle is generally a reliable, but not a sympathetic, witness to developments in the Old Academy, although there appears to be a degree of Schadenfreude in Aristotle's depiction of uncle and nephew holding mutually incompatible doctrines.[193]

Speusippus clearly rejects the Forms in the manner in which they were propounded by Plato and Aristotle (i.e. he rejected Form-Numbers, just accepting mathematical numbers) – so Aristotle is reliable in this respect – but this does not tell us the whole story.[194] Since Forms cannot be combined, Form-Numbers cannot be combined so that they cannot serve as the basis for calculations; this basis is served by mathematical numbers. Speusippus recognised the difficulties with his uncle's system, attempted to resolve them and, observing the necessity of an overarching paradigmatic cause, found place for this function in the World Soul.[195] Speusippus also saw the need of postulating objects of knowledge and found this in numbers and geometrical figures, rather than Plato's Forms. (However, this is not so divergent from Plato when we consider the mathematical nature Plato attributed to the Forms.) In contrast to the frequently made identification of Good with the One, Speusippus did not attribute 'goodness' to the primal One.[196]

Cherniss' observation on the lack of orthodoxy in the Academy illustrates a different understanding of Platonism from that of the Tübingen School. What I would see as Speusippus' modification (rather than outright rejection) of the Forms is less surprising if one regards the Principles, rather than the Forms, as Plato's central doctrine (and, if we regard radical transcendence as an intrinsic feature of Plato's First Principle, then Speusippus can be considered highly orthodox, even more orthodox than Xenocrates in this instance). Furthermore, if Plato had wished to enforce orthodoxy, he would surely have laid down an official school position in written texts, instead of so often ending his dialogues

---

[192] On the development of Platonism from the works of Plato, see Gerson 2005 and 2013.

[193] Dillon 2003: 50 describes Aristotle as 'wickedly misleading'; his reconstruction of Speusippus' metaphysics convincingly demonstrates how Speusippus' doctrines develop out of those of his uncle, rather than constituting a rejection of them.

[194] Dillon 2003: 49 presents Speusippus' activity as a rationalisation of, rather than as an abandonment of, the Forms.

[195] Dillon 2003: 48.   [196] See Dillon 2003: 53.

in *aporia*. Rather, as Dillon has demonstrated, the real legacy he bequeathed to his successors was a 'method of inquiry' which might lead each individually to the truth.[197]

Speusippus' account of the One's nature, as well as his views on the need for a second principle of multiplicity/indeterminacy, is essential for understanding Plotinus' metaphysics. Although John Rist opposed this view, presenting Speusippus as a dualist whose views had limited influence on Neoplatonism, his arguments are not convincing in light of Dillon's and Halfwassen's research, as well as the following fragment of Speusippus (see the discussion at Section 3.6):[198]

> They [sc. the Pythagoreans, the school to which Plato's Theory of Principles is here attributed] supposed that the One is exalted beyond Being and above the 'place from' of Being, and, accordingly, they have freed it from the relationship-determination as a Principle. However, since they judge that nothing comes about from other things, if one contemplates the One itself alone in itself, without any further determinations, pure in itself without adding to it any second element, they brought in the Indefinite Dyad as a Principle of Being. (Speusippus in Proclus, *In Parm.* VII 40, 1–5 Klibansky-Labowsky = Speusippus, Fr. 62 Isnardi Parente = *TP* 50 Gaiser)

There have been attempts to refute Halfwassen's argument by claiming that the Speusippus fragment[199] is a Neopythagorean forgery and not an accurate record.[200] To my mind, this is not a cogent refutation of Halfwassen's position: the description of the One is reminiscent of *Parm.* 143a6–143a8, and the entirety of the fragment reflects a significant concern on the part of Speusippus to connect his own views with those of the Pythagoreans.[201] It would be difficult to conceive of this as an addition of Proclus', since he viewed himself as a *Platonist*, not a *Pythagorean*.[202] (The real oddity is why Speusippus is named at this point.)[203] The passage confirms that Speusippus interpreted the *Parmenides* in the same manner as certain later Platonists, which does not undermine its Old Academic provenance.[204] Steel relies on this similarity to *Parm.* 143a6–143a8 (and Aristotle *Met.* 1081b24–1081b25) to argue against an

---

[197] Dillon 2003: 16.
[198] Rist 1962: 390. Rist's line of interpretation (e.g. 397) avoids attributing significance to the Unwritten Doctrines by deriving Eudorus' views – evidence for the inner-Academic tradition – from a combination of the *Philebus* and misunderstanding Pythagorean doctrines.
[199] Transmitted only in William of Moerbeke's Latin translation.
[200] Notably by Steel 2002, although Steel's challenge was rejected by Gerson 2016: 76; cf. Halfwassen 2006: 365–366, 380–381.
[201] Dillon 2003: 56n62, 153. [202] Halfwassen 2006: 365.
[203] On this, see Dillon 2003: 56n61, 57–58. [204] Cf. Gerson 2016: 76.

Old Academic provenance, although as Halfwassen has demonstrated, this actually supports the opposing claim.[205]

The other main argument running counter to Halfwassen's position (that Plotinus' metaphysics reflect Plato's Theory of Principles) is to claim that Aristotle's report refers to Forms on the level of Intellect, rather than a One 'beyond Being'.[206] Simplicius in his *Commentary on the Physics* already highlighted Aristotle's use of the term 'principles' to refer interchangeably to principles, elements/elementary principles, and causes, rather than exclusively denoting the One and Indefinite Dyad.[207] Simplicius still reads Aristotle as in harmony with Plato regarding the principles of physics, for example, as being subalternate to those of Aristotle's first philosophy (47,19–32), which Simplicius equates with Plato's dialectic (49,3–11) and thereby positions other 'principles' as subordinate to the unhypothetical First Principle of all (*Rep.* VI 511b6–511b7).[208] Now, clearly one can argue that Simplicius, given that he was writing after the closure of the Academy in 529 CE, is of limited value as a witness for Aristotle. Yet it indicates that while he observed Aristotle's differing use of the term 'principle' – something which evidently bothered him enough to treat the matter at some length – he still attempted to demonstrate a continuity in the treatment of the principles, extending via Aristotle and Plato back even to Presocratic accounts (see *In Phys*. 1.2–4).[209] For this reason, it is difficult to rely on Simplicius to refute Halfwassen's view that Plotinus' metaphysics essentially represents the continuity of Plato's Theory of Principles.[210]

A further (related) difficulty is whether Aristotle is entirely consistent in his presentation of the principles. For example, on certain occasions Aristotle identifies the Indefinite Dyad with matter. This identification could be employed to refute Halfwassen's claim that Plotinus' metaphysics reflect a continuity with Plato's Theory of Principles since for Plotinus matter, as the last product of the procession from the One, is clearly not a principle. Again, this does not undermine Halfwassen's position: Plotinus associates matter with indefiniteness and unlimitedness (features associated with the Indefinite Dyad also).[211] More significantly, at *Enn.* II 4 [12], Plotinus introduces intelligible matter which he identifies with the Indefinite Dyad (*Enn.* V 9 [5], 5).[212]

---

[205] Steel 2002; Halfwassen 2006: 382n106.
[206] Luna 2000: 244–245 argues that Syrianus denies a similarity in nature between the Forms and the Principles. Cf. D'Ancona 2000 for historical background.
[207] Sorabji 2012: 1.   [208] For a more detailed discussion, see Menn 2022: 41.
[209] See also Menn 2022: 55.
[210] In any case, Simplicius (245,26–30) attributes a theory of two principles to Plato. Sorabji 2012: 3.
[211] Cf. *Enn.* I 8 [51] 3, 13–16.   [212] Nikulin 2019: 96, 100.

A consequence of the One's radical transcendence is the necessity of this second principle to allow for the constitution of Being.[213] We can even demonstrate that this interpretation, followed by Plotinus, does not simply go back to Speusippus, but to Plato himself. Not only does the One 'beyond Being' refer to *Rep.* VI 509b, but Halfwassen has demonstrated the verbatim correspondence between this passage and the first two hypotheses of the *Parmenides*.[214] The first hypothesis posits a One alone and pure in itself (i.e. without further determinations), while the second hypothesis assigns the second principle a role in the derivation of unity.

Even Aristotle's famous criticism of Speusippus' metaphysics – that his 'episodic universe' resembled a bad tragedy[215] – highlights the influence on him of Plato's Theory of Principles. Speusippus posited a principle of numbers, one of geometric dimension and a principle of soul. It is this which led to him being roundly attacked by Aristotle on the grounds that this universe lacked connections between the various levels. Aristotle is clearly being tendentious here: the various levels are all ultimately derived from the One which provides his ontology with unity at the highest level. Furthermore, Speusippus' speculations allow him to posit multiple ontological levels from the interaction of the two principles (rather than limiting him to a single level).[216]

The interaction of the One and Multiplicity (*plēthos*), his term for what is essentially the Indefinite Dyad, produces Number (or more accurately a 'first principle of number', a 'one' rather than the First Principle, the One) 'by reason of some pervasive Necessity', *DCMS* 4 (p. 15, 17 Festa), an explicit reference to the Necessity of *Tim.* 48a.[217] Natural numbers (or possibly just the Decad, which holds special significance in Pythagorean systems), are produced by the interaction of this 'one', the principle of number and Multiplicity, as well as a principle of geometrical entities: the point (*stigmē*) or principle of Figure.[218] One of these geometric entities unites with a version of Multiplicity to produce Soul, which both generates individual souls and serves as the principle of the physical realm.[219] Even if the details of Speusippus' ontology differ from that of his uncle, we can still see him addressing a feature which Plato had identified as central to metaphysics: the explanation of how multiplicity is derived from

---

[213] Halfwassen 2021: 184, 230. Halfwassen 2006: 381 highlights the significance of this testimonium as the only evidence for why Plato posited a principle of multiplicity.
[214] Halfwassen 2021: 230–231. First hypothesis (137c–142a); second hypothesis (142b–155e).
[215] *Met.* 1028b21–1028b24 (Fr. 29a Tarán), 1075b37–1076a4 (Fr. 30), 1090b13–1090b21 (Fr. 37). Cf. Dillon 2003: 46; Halfwassen 2015: 202.
[216] For reconstructions of Speusippus' metaphysical system, see Dillon 2003: 43–64; Halfwassen 2015: 201–206.
[217] As noted by Dillon 2003: 44. [218] Aristotle, *Met.* 1085a31–1085b4 (= Fr. 51 Tarán).
[219] The details of Speusippus' metaphysics are not as clear as we would like.

unity. This did, however, open Speusippus up to criticism from Aristotle, who claims that Speusippus tried to make his principle of number into the First Principle: Speusippus' vulnerability here is caused by positing three types of one: One/Unity (the First Principle), 'one'/Unit (the principle of number), and one (for Speusippus, as for us, but not for Plato and Aristotle, the first odd number).[220]

This entire series of metaphysical speculations can be understood only within the context of Plato's Theory of Principles as a core feature of inner-Academic teaching. Dillon has demonstrated the extent to which Speusippus' scheme can be viewed as an attempt to deal with difficulties in the system of two principles which he inherited from Plato.[221] Logically, two principles would generate only a single ontological level; Speusippus' system turns the resulting product of the two principles into a kind of further principle which can then combine with one of its generating principles and explain additional levels of Being. Aristotle's attack (at 1085a8–1086a1) on Platonists deriving geometrical entities (such as lines, planes, and solids) from *eidē* (species) of the Great and Small (which implies that he is not referring to Speusippus who termed his second principle Multiplicity) indicates that other successors of Plato were grappling with this problem which he had bequeathed them. In turn, this suggests that – *pace* Cherniss – systematising the Theory of Principles was a focus of intellectual activity at the Academy.

It is not that the Tübingen School has presented a radically new account of Plato that dismembers the dialogues in order to harmonise them with Aristotle's testimonia; this is the sort of account of the Tübingen School which we find in Cherniss, for example. Rather, here we have clear evidence for the recovery of the Theory of Principles traceable in this fragment via the Old Academy, not just to Plato himself, but, in this case, even to specific passages of Plato. Can we really ignore the evidence of Speusippus, who must surely have been better placed than we are to know the intentions of his uncle? Proclus cites this fragment, clearly aware of the role Speusippus played in what he viewed as Plotinus' return to the historically correct – one might say the only correct – interpretation of the Platonic principles.

4.3 The Principles and Developments in Mathematics

As a result of his interest in Pythagoreanism, as well as mathematical research conducted at the Academy (by Eudoxus, Menaechmus, and Theaetetus), Plato's metaphysics and cosmology are heavily influenced by mathematics.[222] This is

---

[220] Dillon 2003: 51. [221] Dillon 2003: 46.
[222] For a discussion of the influence of mathematics in Plato's principles, see Dillon 2003: 18–20.

illustrated by Plato's postulation of Form-Numbers and the manner in which he regarded the Forms generally as numerical entities and, in cosmology, by the geometric structure of the elements and ordering of the universe in accordance with mathematical series. For this reason, if we deny the existence of the Theory of Principles, it is well-nigh impossible to understand the development of mathematics at the Academy.

The numbers are generated from the principles (if we accept the account of Aristotle, *Met.* 1081b10–1081b35; see the discussion on Plotinus in Section 4.4). The primal numbers (the tetraktys: numbers one to four) are generated in the course of determinacy being imposed on the Dyad as a result of its interaction with the One. The interaction between the primal numbers and the Dyad produces the rest of the natural numbers with the Decad (the numbers up to ten) being particularly prominent.

Speusippus, as noted, derives a first principle of number from the interaction between the One and Multiplicity, the natural numbers from the interaction of Multiplicity and this first principle of number, as well as the various principles of extension through space (the first principle of geometrical entities and the first principle of Soul and, ultimately, the physical world). We have already seen the value of this system from an ontological perspective (the derivation of multiple levels from only two principles). However, the connection between mathematics and metaphysics reveals what Krämer described as 'the unified structure of Platonic philosophy'.[223] The Form-Numbers allow the relationship of the universals to each other to be expressed in mathematical terms.[224] This reinforces the interpretation of the Forms being placed in a hierarchical relationship with each other, rather than the collection of free-floating Forms characteristic of Cherniss' conception of the theory.

The reduction of everything to the two ultimate principles is clearly based upon mathematics, although, as Krämer notes, one should not conceive of the Theory of Principles as 'mathematical'.[225] Rather, Plato posits the principles as the ultimate foundation of every sphere (including mathematics), as well as explaining the generation of everything in terms of the interaction of unity and multiplicity (or determinacy and indeterminacy).[226] The principles provide unity to the multiplicity of the Forms, just as the Forms provide unity to the multiplicity of their instantiations in the physical world.[227]

---

[223] The title of chapter 6 in Krämer 1990. [224] See Krämer 1990: 79. [225] Krämer 1990: 82.
[226] Krämer 1990: 83–84.
[227] Halfwassen 2021: 33 provides an extensive list of relevant passages in support: *Rep.* V 476a, 479a; VI 507b; X 596a; *Parm.* 131b–131c, 132a–132d, 133b, 135b–135d; *Phlb.* 15a–b, as well as Aristotle, *Met.* 990b7–990b13, 1079a3–1079a9; *APo* 77a5.

4.4 Plotinus

It is really Halfwassen who did most to highlight the significance of the Tübingen School's approach for understanding Plotinus.[228] It is Plotinus who marks the return to interpreting Plato entirely on the basis of his Theory of Principles; a feature of Platonism which disappeared after the Old Academy.[229] Now a legitimate objection might be raised that just because Plotinus posits principles, these do not necessarily correspond (or correspond entirely) with the principles which are attributed to Plato. Yet Halfwassen has demonstrated the extent to which Plotinus understood the reasons for Plato positing these principles:[230] 'It is because of the One that all beings are beings,[231] both those that are primarily beings and those which are said, in any manner, to be among beings. For what thing could be, if it were not one? For if the oneness which is attributed to things is removed, they are not those things' (*Enn.* VI 9 [9], 1, 1–4).[232]

Intellect, according to Plotinus, can be conceived in terms of the relationship between the One and the Indefinite Dyad (*Enn.* V 4 [7] 2, 7–9): 'On account of this, it is said that the Forms and Numbers – that is Intellect – are derived from the Indefinite Dyad and the One'.[233] The structure of Plotinus' Intellect, consisting of both unity and self-division, can be understood from Plato's Theory of Principles.[234] The primacy Plotinus attributes to the One illustrates his monistic interpretation of the Principles: 'For prior to the Dyad is the One and the Dyad is second and, having its source from the One, the One imposes determinacy on it, but it is itself Indefinite' (*Enn.* V 1 [10] 5, 7–8).

Halfwassen identified three features of Plotinus' understanding of Plato's Theory of Principles; these correspond closely to the Tübingen conception of Plato's original theory.[235]

1. The absolute transcendence of the One 'beyond Being' (as indicated by *Rep.* VI 509b). The observation that the One is beyond Being has further consequences: 'For since it is beyond Being, it is beyond activity and beyond Intellect and thought' (*Enn.* I 7 [54] 1, 19–21) – that is, a rejection of Xenocrates' equation of the First Principle with Intellect.[236]

---

[228] See also Krämer 1964a: 163–369.
[229] Halfwassen 2015: 150. This is noted by both Proclus (*Theol. Plat.* I 1, 6, 16–21) and Ficino. See Halfwassen 2021: 178–179.
[230] Most significantly Halfwassen 2015.
[231] The Greek can be read both as 'because of unity' and 'because of the One'.
[232] See Halfwassen 2015: 149 for a discussion of this passage.
[233] Halfwassen 2015: 158; cf. *Enn.* III 8 [30] 11, 5–6; V 3 [49] 5, 43–44; VI 6 [34] 9, 29–34; Aristotle, *Met.* 987b21–987b22, 1081a13–1081a15.
[234] On this and the influence of *Parmenides* 157e–158d, see Halfwassen 2015: 159–160. Cf. *Enn.* VI 2 [43] 3, 21–32.
[235] Halfwassen 2015: 150 and 2021: 179–180.
[236] See Halfwassen 2021: 44.

2. The monism of the First Principle and consequent subordination of the principle of multiplicity to the One.
3. The absolute Intellect (as the totality of the Forms) is constituted from the determination of the principle of multiplicity by the One.[237] Note how this differs both from attempts to claim the Idea of the Good as the totality of the Forms or attempts by Xenocrates to identify the First Principle with Intellect and to position the Forms as the contents of this Intellect.

Plotinus' exegesis of Plato can be considered an articulation of the Theory of Principles.

Another characteristic feature of Neoplatonism, *ecstasis* (ἔκστασις, 'standing outside oneself'), the mystical process that permits the soul's ascent to the One, is a consequence of the One's absolute transcendence. Since the One is beyond Intellect and beyond thought, there needs to be another mechanism for ascending to the One (which is provided by ecstasis). Halfwassen highlights the significance of this for our understanding of Plotinus: mysticism is not the starting point of his philosophy, but a consequence of the transcendence of the One, resulting from his actual starting point, Plato's Theory of Principles.[238] Plotinian mysticism is based upon an accurate interpretation of Plato's metaphysics and actually a consequence of this interpretation. This highlights once more the significance of the Tübingen School's approach for our understanding of the history of philosophy.

4.5 Proclus

Proclus explicitly claims the Unwritten Doctrines, constituting the Theory of the Principles, as the core element of Plato's theology while also testifying to the oral dissemination of this theory within the Old Academy. He reveals himself to be an accurate historian of philosophy when he both regards Plotinus as representing a break with the Platonism which immediately preceded it,[239] and sees him as returning to Plato's Theory of Principles. Speusippus' interpretation of Plato's *Parmenides* presents an exegesis of the Theory of Principles which corresponds to Plotinus' exegesis of the principles, a fact which did not escape the notice of Proclus.[240]

Of course, we are not obliged simply to accept Proclus' interpretation of the history of Platonism. Yet it should be clear that Schleiermacheanism has obscured this tradition: the Theory of Principles, forming the core of Plato's

---

[237] This was seen by Krämer 1964a. Cf. Halfwassen 2021: 188n32.
[238] Halfwassen 2021: 41, supported by *Enn.* VI 9 [9] 4.
[239] I.e. what we now refer to as Middle Platonism.
[240] Proclus, *In Parm.* VII, pp. 38, 32–40, 7 Klibansky. Dillon 2003: 57 suggests either Porphyry's or Iamblichus' *Commentary on the Parmenides* as Proclus' source. Cf. Halfwassen 2021: 229–232.

philosophy, was transmitted via Speusippus (although the provenance of this theory was already backdated by the Old Academy to the Pythagoreans) and fell out of favour during Middle Platonism, which was dominated by Xenocrates, before re-emerging again under Plotinus, a fact recognised by Proclus.

5 Critics of the Unwritten Doctrines

5.1 Schleiermacher, His Followers, and Other 'Anti-esoterics'

While some of the arguments against the Tübingen School's position have been mentioned previously, it is worth turning now to a more detailed examination of whether these form a cogent refutation – and, to this end, in this section, I adopt the most sympathetic and persuasive reading of each argument against the Tübingen position.[241] The Tübingen School appears to have resolved numerous perplexing issues with reading Plato. Even if we reject its approach, the problems they identified still require a solution.

The main opposition (historically) to the notion of Unwritten Doctrines can be referred to as Schleiermacheanism, arising from Schleiermacher's introduction to his translation of Plato's dialogues (1804), advocating for a literal interpretation of the dialogues. I use Schleiermacheanism to refer to the views of both the founding father and his disciples in North America, notably Shorey, Cherniss, and Vlastos. Non-Schleiermacheans (other 'anti-esoterics') who reject the Tübingen approach are treated separately in what follows.[242] Schleiermacheanism left no room for the indirect tradition, which had been significant for the study of Plato, until its recovery by the Tübingen School (although even immediately this weakness of Schleiermacher's theory was exposed by Böckh and, subsequently, by Friedrich Adolf Trendelenburg).[243] Trendelenburg even connected the Unwritten Doctrines with the *Philebus*.[244]

Several predecessors of the Tübingen–Milan School paved the way for the recovery of the Unwritten Doctrines:[245] among them Robin in France, who argued for the significance of the indirect tradition;[246] the German scholar Ulrich von Wilamovitz-Moellendorff (1848–1931), who defended the *Seventh Letter* as authentic;[247] and, in Austria, Heinrich Gomperz (1873–1942), who

---

[241] For example, the responses of Mackenzie 1982 and Rowe 1986 to the *Phaedrus*' criticism of writing since they take it seriously and adopt thoughtful responses to it.
[242] I am borrowing the term 'anti-esoteric' from Gaiser 1980: 7.
[243] Böckh [1808] 1872: 5–9; Trendelenburg 1826; Krämer 1990: 29–30.
[244] See Krämer 1990: 30. [245] Krämer 1990: 38–41 provides a detailed account.
[246] Robin 1908: 499–584.
[247] Wilamovitz-Moellendorff 1919: 2:281 notes that he previously regarded the *Seventh Letter* as spurious on the grounds that it was not Plato's manner to speak about himself, but changed his opinion on the basis of a deeper understanding of Plato's thought (281–282). See Wilamovitz-Moellendorff 1919: 2:282–300 for his analysis of the *Seventh Letter*.

built on the work of Robin and acceptance of the *Seventh Letter*'s authenticity in identifying the One of the testimonia with the Idea of the Good in the *Republic*.[248] This refutes the impression that Schleiermacheanism, even before the objections raised against it by Krämer and Gaiser, was universally accepted.

Schleiermacheanism can be defined in a basic sense as a belief in the autonomy of the literary dialogues, which consequently comes to represent the entirety of Plato's philosophy, thereby eliminating any role for the oral/indirect tradition.[249] Schleiermacher was correct in asserting the central role of the *Phaedrus* for understanding all of Plato's works (although, unfortunately, he pushed this insight in the wrong direction by not regarding the doubts expressed in the dialogue as valid for Plato's own compositions and, instead, regarded the *Phaedrus* as programmatic for Plato's attempts to avoid the shortcomings of writing which he identified). It should be noted that Schleiermacher, in contrast to many other opponents of the Tübingen School (such as Shorey and Cherniss), left the status of the *Seventh Letter* as an open question. Schleiermacher even recognised the significance of the Idea of the Good, although this has been downplayed by some of his followers.[250]

In the English-speaking world, Schleiermacher's approach is most closely associated with Shorey, who was influenced by Schleiermacheanism – particularly through Eduard Zeller's (1814–1908) mediation of it – in the course of his doctoral studies at Munich;[251] with Cherniss, who completed his doctorate with Shorey's student R. M. Jones at Chicago; and with Vlastos.[252]

It is helpful to examine the points which both sides regard as incontrovertible:

1. The Idea of the Good is clearly assigned a central role in the *Republic*, although Plato's dialogues do not explicitly identify the Good with the One.[253]
2. The dialogues do not (explicitly) posit a second principle, the Indefinite Dyad. Claims that Plato posited such a principle draw largely on sources from the Platonic tradition. For the Tübingen School, though, several passages of the *Parmenides* can be cited in support of this principle, even if not employing the name 'Indefinite Dyad' (e.g. *Parm.* 142d–143a, 158b–158c, 159d–160b, 164c8–164d1); these passages deal with a plurality (165e1) or

---

[248] Gomperz 1931: 159, 163–164. Gomperz also rejects the Good being regarded as just an Idea and correctly identifies the significance of the *Philebus* for understanding Plato's philosophical system.

[249] Krämer 1990: 38, with a fuller definition of the six characteristics shared by Schleiermacher's followers, Shorey and Cherniss, at Krämer 1990: 36.

[250] On Schleiermacher's notion of Plato's system, see Krämer 1990: 22.

[251] See Krämer 1990: 34–35 for an account of Shorey's intellectual development.

[252] The intellectual genealogy of the prominent North American Schleiermacheans is traced by Krämer 1990: 34.

[253] Gerson 2014: 398.

'others than the one' (165c5).²⁵⁴ It is also evident that there must be a separate cause or causes for bad things (*Rep.* II 379c5–379c6), which suggests that there must be a second principle. The Receptacle (χώρα) of the *Timaeus* can be viewed as such a cause.²⁵⁵
3. Plato's Socrates criticises writing in the *Phaedrus*, but the exact scope and range of this criticism are open to debate.

While Cherniss reads the role which the *Republic* assigns to the Idea of the Good as hyperbole and, like Shorey, undermines its metaphysical significance, more recent scholars outside the Schleiermachean orbit (notably Julia Annas, Broadie, and Penner), although not accepting the Tübingen line of interpretation, have seriously attempted to engage with some of the issues raised by the Tübingen approach regarding the Good.²⁵⁶ Such interaction has proven fruitful and these scholars offer significantly more coherent non-Tübingen readings than the Schleiermacheans.

Penner suggests that the Idea of the Good is the Form of Advantage or Benefit, outlined as Plato's attempt to find a 'global theory of Good',²⁵⁷ rather than moral or absolute Good.²⁵⁸ Although I am not convinced by this reading – viewing it as bearing traces of the tendency to downplay the centrality of the Idea of the Good exhibited by Shorey and Cherniss – I can see why Penner was motivated to suggest it. A major difficulty of the *Republic* is seeing how the Idea of the Good – which is investigated in the manner of a digression from the exploration of justice in the soul and polis – can be relevant to the philosopher-kings. Aristotle identifies this problem at *NE* 1097a8, when he notes that it is difficult to envisage how viewing this Idea will make one a better general or doctor or carpenter.²⁵⁹ This difficulty is magnified by the lack of details supplied concerning the exact constitution of the Idea of the Good.²⁶⁰ Notably, Penner also concludes that the 'longer road' is started upon, but not pursued until the end (which sounds rather like a deliberate gap, even if this terminology is not employed).²⁶¹

---

²⁵⁴ Szlezák 1999: 608–612 provides an extensive analysis of *Parmenides* passages which have been regarded as postulating an Indefinite Dyad.
²⁵⁵ Szlezák 1999: 613 considers the extent to which the Receptacle can be regarded as a variant of the Dyad.
²⁵⁶ See Cherniss 1936; Gerson: 2014: 401–402. Similarly, Penner 2007a: 33 refers to *Rep.* VI 509a9–509c2, the passage outlining the analogy of the sun, as 'too airily metaphysical'.
²⁵⁷ Penner 2007a: 35.
²⁵⁸ Penner 2007a: 31. Penner 2007a: 24, 34 notes that the 'longer road' has not received much serious attention from scholars, although it has since been extensively treated by Szlezák 2019a: 343–357.
²⁵⁹ See Annas 1999: 96, 115.
²⁶⁰ Rowe 2007: 125; Seel 2007: 168. Outside the Tübingen tradition, Rowe 2007a: 125 highlights that the elements of the Good in the *Republic* can be understood from other dialogues (e.g. *Lysis*), a view asserted also by the Tübingen School.
²⁶¹ Penner 2007a: 36.

Rowe raises a more general difficulty with an approach adopted by Platonists of a range of persuasions – 'cherry-picking'.[262] For our purposes, the relevant claim that Rowe raises is the reliance on *Rep.* VI 509b to demonstrate that the Good is 'beyond Being' without any demonstration that, of all the comments on the Good in the dialogues, this particular passage should be taken as 'foundational'.[263] Against this, I would argue that this is part of the tendency to marginalise the Theory of Principles and that the Tübingen School does not fall victim to the tendency of 'cherry-picking'. While the passage is particularly significant for the Tübingen School's viewpoint, it simply reinforces indications of the existence of the Unwritten Doctrines found across a range of dialogues.

5.2 Aristotle's Reliability as a Witness to Plato

The difficulty of rejecting Aristotle's account was pointedly formulated by Trendelenburg: 'If Aristotle, a man of such talents and on intimate terms with Plato for so many years, did not know [sc. how to interpret Plato], who else would know it?'[264] Cherniss' view was that Aristotle misinterpreted the written dialogues and that this is what triggered belief in Unwritten Doctrines not reflected in the texts.[265] Aristotle and Plato did not always enjoy a particularly harmonious relationship: Aristotle referred to Plato's Forms as 'meaningless chatter' (*APo* 83a33) and described his Theory of Principles as 'illogical' (*Met.* 1091a6)[266] and 'not reasonable' (*Met.* 988a1–2).[267] If we accept an anecdote from Aelian's *Varia Historia* (3.19), Aristotle's aggressive interrogation of the elderly Plato (during the absence of Xenocrates and illness of Speusippus) even forced Plato to abandon the Academy grove temporarily.[268]

Aristotle's reliability as a witness is certainly a major point of contention between the Tübingen School and its opponents. For the Tübingen School, it provides evidence of the oral tradition, allowing us to understand how Plato's dialogues can be interpreted. For the Schleiermacheans, Aristotle's dismissal would remove one line of argumentation (but not the only line of argumentation) for the Theory of Principles. This criticism of Aristotle as a witness goes back to an early follower of Schleiermacher, Zeller. Cherniss' argument is that Aristotle's testimonies must be subjected to the 'control' of the dialogues.[269] The difficulty for the opponents of Tübingen is that, much as in the case of the

---

[262] Rowe 2014: 7–8. [263] Rowe 2014: 7.
[264] 'Quod si nescivisset Aristoteles, tanti ingenii vir, per tot annos Platoni familiaris – quis tandem sciret?', Trendelenburg 1826, 3. Cf. Cherniss 1945: 9; Hösle 2019: 334–335.
[265] Cherniss 1945: 29; Cf. Sayre 2005: 79.
[266] Particularly the generation of number from the One and Indefinite Dyad.
[267] Cf. Sayre 2005: 83, 284n21. [268] Dillon 2003: 3–4; O'Brien and Wear 2017: 255.
[269] Cherniss 1945: 20; cf. Gerson 2014: 307.

Seventh Letter, whether we accept this testimony or not, the same arguments for the Tübingen position can be advanced, supported by other evidence.

An excellent example of Cherniss' approach is illustrated by his analysis of the debate concerning the *Timaeus* among Plato's students. The *Timaeus* famously depicts the generation of the world by a Craftsman-god (Demiurge), but suggests that the world is everlasting at the pleasure of the Demiurge. Many Greek philosophers would have regarded this as an illogical approach: either the world is generated in time and subject to dissolution (as in Stoicism) or it is eternal (without beginning or end). It is more difficult to support the view of a world that has a temporal beginning, but no end. This led to a debate within the Platonic circle of whether Plato intended the *Timaeus* account literally.[270] Aristotle argues for the literal interpretation, whereas Xenocrates claimed that the Demiurge myth was merely 'for the purpose of exposition' (*didaskalias charin*, Fr. 54).

We can see a similarity in Aristotle's treatment of the Receptacle in the *Timaeus*.[271] Essentially the Receptacle is described by Plato as a 'third kind' (*Tim.* 48e4) and 'space', although it seems to combine characteristics of matter and space. Now Aristotle is unable to ascertain if Plato's treatment of the Receptacle and his account of the elementary triangles are incompatible since the *Timaeus* does not clearly state whether the Receptacle and the elements are separate.[272] Cherniss draws several inferences about the status of teaching in the Academy from Aristotle's expressed confusion concerning the Receptacle, arguing that Plato did not offer any further exegesis to his students beyond what was supplied in the dialogues.[273]

The question why it never occurred to Aristotle to ask Plato what he meant seems – on the face of it – eminently reasonable.[274] The ambiguity whether Plato intended the *Timaeus* myth literally or not – even within Plato's immediate circle – suggests that Plato's views rested on what was presented in the dialogues and casts doubt not only on whether there was any teaching on the Unwritten Doctrines, but whether any teaching whatsoever was supplied in the Academy. It may simply be the case that Plato never committed to any specific view in his teaching – much like the situation in the dialogues – since the most significant elements of his philosophy require the student being led along to this insight, rather than simply being informed about it.[275]

---

[270] For a fuller account of this, see O'Brien 2015: 26–29.
[271] Cherniss 1944: 150 and 1945: 72.
[272] Aristotle, *De Generatione* 329a8–329a24, especially the criticism that Plato, *Tim.* 49d–50a is not based on a precisely articulated conception.
[273] Cherniss 1944: 165 and 1945: 72.   [274] Cherniss 1945: 71.
[275] Rowe 2014: 4 supplies a range of reasons for why Plato may never have offered his own opinion.

Cherniss then suggests that German philologists envisage Plato's Academy as something approaching the modern research university, based upon the Humboldtian model, linking this to their cultural background.[276] He himself presents an image of Plato as an 'individual thinker whose insight and skill in the formulation of a problem enables him to offer general insight and methodological criticism', rather than a modern research director or even the head of a school similar to Aristotle's Lyceum.[277] According to him, the Academy can be regarded as something more akin to a *thiasos* (religious fraternity) than the sort of academic institution with which we are familiar.[278]

This move can be seen as parallel to the attempt to dismiss Plato's lecture(s) *On the Good*, but Cherniss does raise a number of significant points. The inferences of the Tübingen School are so important because their consequences go beyond interpretation of the dialogues – itself a major concern – to presenting an insight into the nature of the Academy and the intellectual activity conducted there. However, while Cherniss' line of argumentation certainly appears to be persuasive, a number of weaknesses emerge upon closer analysis. For example, there is, in fact, evidence for regular teaching at the Academy (discussed in what follows).

Cherniss' methodology – the use of the dialogues to 'control' Aristotle's testimony concerning Plato's teaching and to employ this as grounds for excluding Aristotle's testimony in points unable to be 'controlled' by the dialogues, since it appears inaccurate to Cherniss – can be refuted. Aristotle's testimony concerning the dialogues is correct: he does not misrepresent Plato in claiming a literal, rather than a metaphorical, interpretation of the Demiurge myth and his observations on the Receptacle do not distort Plato's thought. Even if his literal reading places the *Timaeus* in the worst possible light, this demonstrates that Aristotle is a reliable – even if a non-sympathetic witness – exactly the opposite of what Cherniss requires to make his case.

Vlastos is at least willing to accept the possibility that Plato had discussed notions such as the Indefinite Dyad, the mathematical Ideas and the Idea numbers within the Academy, although minimalising them as 'attractive enough to merit exposition', but not fully worked out enough to merit publication.[279] This solution, at any rate, has the advantage of not denying the historical record and avoids portraying Aristotle as disingenuous and unreliable – although Vlastos still blames Aristotle for not noting Plato's doubts on this subject. The misleading projection of modern notions (superiority of writing over oral discourse) has

---

[276] Cherniss 1945: 61–62.
[277] Cherniss 1945: 11, 65, although see Krämer's parallels between Plato's and Aristotle's pedagogical practice, discussed later in this section.
[278] Cherniss 1945: 61. [279] Vlastos 1963: 653–654.

already been mentioned. The difficulty is that it still wilfully misunderstands the centrality of the Unwritten Doctrines for Plato's thought as a whole. This is illustrated neatly by Vlastos' dismissal of the entire subject, when he noted that he was 'not convinced that an "esoteric Plato" is one of the burning questions of present-day Platonic scholarship'.[280] In a way, it should not be a 'burning question'; it is only the loss of the indirect tradition due to the dominance of Schleiermacheanism which has obscured the core, not just of Plato's philosophy, but of its historical development in the Old Academy.

5.3 The Significance of the Lecture(s) *On the Good*

Cherniss argues – in an attempt to undermine the significance of the lecture(s) *On the Good* – that our evidence only illustrates that this was a once-off event and that there is simply no proof to support the claim that Plato delivered a systematic course of lectures at the Academy. Cherniss – using the same line of argumentation which he employs to dismiss Aristotle's testimony – maintains that such a supposition involves the imposition of modern pedagogical norms on Plato's 'school' and inference from Aristotle's Lyceum, neither of which can fully justify this claim.[281]

However, we have evidence not just of this famous lecture on the Good, but of a second lecture (or discussion) delivered by Plato at the Academy grove. Admittedly, this comes from Aelian so it is vulnerable to dismissal as a later source.[282] We also have contemporary evidence for how teaching in the Academy might be structured from the dialogues themselves, presented according to a variety of models: dialectic (as depicted across a range of dialogues), one on one tuition in mathematics (*Meno* 82b–85c), and, indeed, a (semi-) formal lecture on a technical subject (cosmology and astronomy),[283] delivered by Timaeus. Further investigation on the pedagogical practices of Plato's Academy would simply carry us too far off topic; my purpose here is limited to demonstrating that Cherniss' assertions of what transpired in the Academy are not supported by the evidence.

A much more serious objection is the question why Plato would choose a public lecture to those unfamiliar with his philosophy as the occasion to discuss the Theory of Principles since it appears strange to present an 'esoteric' doctrine in such a venue.[284] Cherniss claims that Plato ignores his own advice

---

[280] Vlastos 1973: 399 where Vlastos also notes that he has more important matters to attend to than engage in further debate on the Unwritten Doctrines.
[281] Cherniss 1945: 10–11. [282] Aelian, *Varia Historia* 3.19.
[283] I categorise it as semi-formal since the overarching context places it as part of a series of conversations, although Timaeus' speech could easily be characterised as formal.
[284] Cherniss 1945: 11–12.

offered in the criticism of writing at *Phdr.* 274b–278e and undermines the argument that the Theory of Principles is missing from the dialogues because they were intended for the general public. Yet the Theory of Principles is treated in the dialogues (if one accepts the reading that the deliberate gaps note where this theory might be examined in a fuller discussion and the indications concerning the principles in the *Republic* and *Philebus*). The reaction Plato's lecture met with clearly indicates that it was not advisable, but does not run counter to explicit treatment of the principles *in writing* which Plato objected to.

Yet Krämer has addressed the presentation of Plato's disastrous public lecture in a manner which undermines an apparently strong refutation.[285] What is understood as a public lecture may, in fact, not have been public after all, but part of regular instruction at the Academy. (This would undermine attempts to marginalise the lecture by portraying it as a once-off event.) Vlastos uses the element of surprise experienced by the audience as support for the once-off nature of the event, since, he suggests, it is difficult to imagine naive individuals turning up repeatedly only to be subject to the same disappointment.[286] The report of this lecture goes on to note that Aristotle learned from this disaster of Plato's and always supplied an introduction to his lectures so that his listeners – unlike Plato's – were not disappointed.[287] Krämer argues that since Aristotle's courses were regularly repeated and his listeners still seemed unaware of their content, we could envisage Plato's teaching *On the Good* as being regularly repeated.[288]

There are not many scholars working on Plato now who would follow Cherniss' views in their entirety. However, even modern interpretations which do not place the lecture(s) on the Good as central to their thesis (such as Broadie's) still address it. The topic is important since understanding the nature of teaching in the Academy is an issue of perennial interest and it is one area where the fault lines between the Tübingen School and some contemporary 'anti-esoterics' do not appear to be so rigid. For example, both Broadie and Gaiser ultimately do not see it as central to understanding the Good of the *Republic*.[289] Gaiser, in contrast to some of his Tübingen School colleagues, agreed with Cherniss' protests, against the 'expansion of the evidence' to present the lecture as part of regular teaching at the Academy, rather than a single event.[290] Even if the issue of the lecture is less central than it once was, the contradiction between a public lecture on the Good and the reticence advised in the *Seventh Letter* requires an explanation. Gaiser's solution is that the lecture took place after the composition of the *Seventh Letter*,[291] when Plato

---

[285] Krämer 1964b: 140. [286] Vlastos 1963: 650.
[287] Aristoxenus, *Harmonika*, Marquard 44,5. [288] Krämer 1964b: 140.
[289] Gaiser 1980: 7; Broadie 2021: 178n29. [290] Gaiser 1980: 16.
[291] This claim would not convince those who regard the *Seventh Letter* as a later 'forgery'.

decided to present the authentic version of the doctrine to the public, either to counter Dionysius' writings or in response to Athenian hostility to the Academy's esotericism.[292]

5.4 Dismissal of Other Evidence concerning the Unwritten Doctrines

In tandem with dismissing the evidence from Aristotle, opponents of the Unwritten Doctrines also attempt to undermine the reliability of other testimony. Sextus Empiricus' report (*Adv. Math.* X 248–283 = *TP* 32 Gaiser) is a favoured target of Schleiermachean attacks.[293] He attributes a Theory of Principles to the Pythagoreans, which paves the way for attributing this theory to the Old Academy and, ultimately, to Plato himself.[294] Initially, linking Sextus' attribution to the Pythagoreans with Plato might seem like something of a stretch, but Szlezák analyses this in terms of Plato's demonstrated use of camouflage. Just as Plato portrays the Theory of Forms in the dialogues as 'Socratic' (since they are presented by Socrates, although the theory was not held by the historical Socrates), he depicts the Theory of Principles as 'Pythagorean' (presented by Timaeus, a Pythagorean, or 'the ancients', *Philebus* 16c).[295] Sextus is an important source since, if one claims (as Krämer does) that his information is not based on Aristotle's περὶ τἀγαθοῦ (*On the Good*), but instead is transmitted via the inner-Academic tradition, this circumvents much of the opposition to employing Aristotle's testimony and provides independent confirmation of it.[296] Much like the situation with the *Seventh Letter*, Sextus' report actually confirms information available from other sources, so that the Tübingen School position can be constructed without reference to it.[297]

5.5 Reflections on Schleiermacher's Followers

The followers of Schleiermacher try to marginalise both the *Schriftkritik* of the *Phaedrus* and the Theory of Principles, thereby presenting them as separate from the core of Plato's thought (and therefore as something that can be dismissed, rather than as an essential component). It is clear that both doctrines – the criticism of writing and the principles – interact with each other and it is equally

---

[292] Gaiser 1980: 20.
[293] E.g. Vlastos 1963: 644–648, although as Szlezák 1999: 602 notes, not of major significance for Cherniss 1944.
[294] For a persuasive defence of Sextus' report, see Szlezák 1999: 601–614.
[295] Szlezák 1999: 603.
[296] Krämer 1959: 250n11. Sextus' report (*TP* 32, section 261) probably goes back to Xenocrates (cf. Halfwassen 2015: 106), although the six centuries between Plato and Sextus raise the possibility of some distortions in transmission.
[297] On the harmony between Sextus Empiricus' report and the *Parmenides*, see Szlezák 1999: 613–614.

clear that both views can be demonstrated from Plato's middle period.[298] The principles are not a late afterthought, but a central development.[299] For this reason any attempt to marginalise such views can only lead to a misunderstanding of Plato's philosophy.

Part of the reason why the Tübingen School approach has also not found traction is that it entails a revolutionary rethinking, not only of our conception of Plato, but also of what it means to philosophise, to 'do philosophy'. The dominant paradigm envisages that we accomplish this by means of written texts outlining our views (a notion that, in any case, does not fully hold true for Plato's dialogues). Plato's *Cratylus* similarly problematises the value of language (even in oral form) for inquiries into the ultimate nature of reality (which in itself should render the Tübingen position more persuasive).

6 Conclusion

6.1 Are There Advantages to the Tübingen School Approach?

Do the views of the Tübingen School actually improve our understanding of Plato and the wider Platonic tradition? To this, we must respond in the affirmative. First, it accounts for the deliberate gaps in the dialogues and manages to harmonise with what we learn about teaching in the Academy and among Plato's immediate successors. Second, it helps to account for the systematisation of Plato attempted by Speusippus and Xenocrates in terms of the Theory of Principles – otherwise it would be very difficult to understand how these developments relate to Plato's own thought. Third, given the significance of the Theory of Principles for Neoplatonism and following Halfwassen's interpretation, it highlights the continuity of Platonic thought, rather than presenting Neoplatonism as a radical departure from Platonism. This notion of Platonism as a continuity reflects the view held by the Neoplatonists themselves, as well as by George Berkeley (in the *Siris*), and, indeed, was a standard way of conceiving the Platonic tradition until Anton Büsching (1774).[300] I am certainly not advancing the case that just because an appreciation for the oral/indirect tradition has historically been a hallmark of Platonism, that this must always continue. Rather, I wish to counter a sleight of hand by which the Tübingen–Milan approach is represented as a regional curiosity, originating only with Krämer in 1959. In fact, what is now the dominant approach to the study of

---

[298] This is not to say that the Theory of Principles is irrelevant for interpretation of the early dialogues; Krämer 1964b: 164 suggests that the early dialogues can support an ontology of principles.
[299] Vlastos 1963: 654.
[300] This is not intended as an appeal to authority, but rather to highlight the significance of the Theory of Principles for our understanding of the history of philosophy.

Plato – certainly in the English-speaking world – goes back only as far as the publication of Schleiermacher's introduction to his translations in 1804.

Some clarity is needed regarding the proponents of the Unwritten Doctrines. This approach was independently advanced by Findlay (so it is not accurate to describe all of the proponents as members of the Tübingen School). Furthermore, the group does not constitute a monolithic bloc: Reale expressed reservations concerning some aspects of Krämer's approach, such as the limited role of the Demiurge (although these modifications to his position were largely accepted by Krämer subsequently).[301]

The Tübingen–Milan School raises serious challenges to the understanding of Plato presented by Schleiermacheanism. We are, of course, free to reject Tübingen's solutions, but we still need to address the problems raised and it is difficult to do that within a Schleiermachean framework.

1. If Plato's criticism of writing does not apply to his own works, what arguments can we make for ignoring it? (Plato, after all, does not criticise all writing *except dialogues*, he criticises writing itself.) Ignoring the *Schriftkritik* runs counter to the claims made by Schleiermacher of interpreting the dialogues from the text itself.
2. If the deliberate gaps do not refer to Plato's Unwritten Doctrines, what do they refer to? These passages are found so pervasively across several of Plato's more significant dialogues that it is clear that they require some explanation. What could this be?
3. If we ignore the textual evidence, the argument for the Tübingen School's position can be made metaphysically. Plato's Theory of Forms, according to the Schleiermachean approach, simply consists of a series of disconnected universals. Without a hierarchical ordering among the Forms (such as is provided by the Idea of the Good), they appear to lack an overarching unity. The alternative would be to suggest that Plato works out different approaches in different contexts within some kind of shared framework: for example the Good is central to the *Republic*, while Beauty is the highest relevant Form in the *Symposium*. Yet even with such a reading the case can be made for the centrality of the Idea of the Good within Plato's entire system.
4. Related to the preceding point, even Schleiermacheans would find it challenging to deny the centrality of the Good in the *Republic*. If we deny the identification of the Good with the One (which, to be fair to the Schleiermacheans, is not explicitly made in the *Republic*), how are we to understand it? Interpretation of Plato is not well served by dismissing it (like

---

[301] Krämer 1986; Reale 1990: xxv and 2010.

Cherniss) simply as a 'hyperbolic joke' (although today this is by no means a mainstream view).[302] Other scholars who reject the identification of the Good as One and prefer to see it in terms of Advantage or Benefit (notably Penner and Rowe) still take the nature of its role in the *Republic* as a question worthy of serious study.

5. If we choose to ignore textual and metaphysical arguments, the Tübingen School position could still be reconstructed from the history of philosophy. Granted, just because other Platonists believed something is not a reason for why we should do so too and they clearly diverged among themselves: Speusippus rejected (or, more accurately, rationalised) the Forms, Xenocrates argued for a non-literal interpretation of the Demiurge myth, while his own student, Crantor of Soli, was in favour of interpreting Plato literally, so that Xenocrates' apprenticeship and direct acquaintance with Plato does not seem to have carried much weight with his own student. It is clear that the testimonia elucidate both Plato's own dialogues, as well as developments in the Old Academy, which is certainly an argument in favour of accepting them. Our resultant understanding of Neoplatonism as a continuity of the Platonic tradition, rather than as a radical departure, while not itself an argument for adopting the Unwritten Doctrines, is an important consequence.

6. Schleiermacheans can legitimately attack the authenticity of the *Seventh Letter*. Yet even conceding for the sake of argument that the *Seventh Letter* is inauthentic – and personally, I do not believe that the *Seventh Letter* is by Plato – this does not necessarily mean that it has no philosophical value. Furthermore, the *Seventh Letter* expresses one particular reaction to the use of writing which is discussed in more general terms in the *Phaedrus*. So the *Seventh Letter* does not supply arguments on this topic which we cannot find elsewhere in the corpus and we can advance the same line of argumentation without appealing to the *Seventh Letter* in any case.

There are numerous methodological flaws in the Schleiermachean approach. First, there is absolutely no justification for the application of Protestant biblical hermeneutics to Plato's dialogues, particularly given the very different nature of Plato's corpus and the Bible. The tenet of *sola scriptura* runs counter to the historically predominant method of interpreting Plato and, given the significance of the indirect tradition and Plato's express misgivings about outlining the entirety of his thought within these works, it is clear both why this historically was not the dominant interpretative approach and that such a mode of interpreting Plato could only produce a misleading understanding of his thought. Since classical texts

---

[302] To employ the phrasing of Gerson 2014: 402. Cf. Cherniss 1936.

require expounding within their original cultural and intellectual context, *sola scriptura* runs counter to the very discipline of classical philology; the text should not be read on its own and in a vacuum. It should be noted that two particular weaknesses of the Schleiermachean approach like dating the *Phaedrus* to the start of Plato's literary activity and the dismissal of the Idea of the Good as a joke are not taken seriously nowadays.[303] As a result, more recent scholars who hold non-Tübingen views (notably Broadie and Penner) have produced much more coherent accounts of the role of the Good in the *Republic*, even while rejecting its identification as the One.

Even if we reject the solutions of the Tübingen School, these scholars make a serious attempt to resolve the difficulties of Plato's texts and to produce a coherent thesis based upon a consistently applied methodology, relying on textual analysis of both Plato's dialogues and the testimonia, as well as metaphysical reasoning, something Schleiermacheanism fails to achieve. Schleiermacheanism's lack of a coherent methodology is illustrated by its insistence on solely reading the dialogues, then ignoring passages which its notion of Plato cannot explain, by dismissing Aristotle's testimony, but then drawing upon Aristotle when his evidence suits its arguments. Gerson, one of the most distinguished contemporary Platonists in North America, is correct when he refers to the influence of Cherniss (1944) as 'largely baleful'. This is not to deny the erudition of Cherniss, which Gerson acknowledges, but it is difficult to construct a solid edifice upon a shaky methodological foundation.[304] The ascent of Schleiermacheanism has led to the loss of one of the great currents of Platonic thought, the oral/indirect tradition.

6.2 Research Questions Highlighted by the Unwritten Doctrines

Vlastos dismissed the significance of the Unwritten Doctrines as a research topic.[305] Yet the Tübingen School's work has repercussions for several questions which are key to our understanding of Plato.

1. What is the purpose and function of the Platonic dialogues and who was their intended readership? This is clearly impacted by the notion that the core of Plato's philosophy was conveyed orally (i.e. outside the dialogues); a means of philosophical instruction outside the dialogues is consequently necessary, raising the possibility that the dialogues were intended as advertising to attract potential students.
2. What sort of teaching went on in the Old Academy? What was the relationship of this course of instruction to what was depicted in the dialogues?

---

[303] See Cherniss 1945: 10–11, 20, 57, 60.   [304] Gerson 2014: 408.
[305] Vlastos 1973: 399, discussed in Section 5.

3. Related to the first two points, how should we read the Platonic dialogues? Clearly the *Phaedrus'* criticism of writing, the dialogue's intended readership, the extent to which Plato reveals (or does not reveal) the core of his philosophy within the dialogues themselves and the extent to which it is prudent to interpret Plato from other sources all impact how we read his corpus.

Section 5 provided an overview of the Schleiermachean position and considered the evidence for rejecting the Tübingen School approach. Even if we were to accept Schleiermacheanism, it would leave us unable to account for numerous problems for which the Tübingen School has a response.

1. If we reject the *Phaedrus' Schriftkritik*, we either have to opt for Schleiermacher's misleading chronology or claim that Platonic dialogues are exempt from this criticism. This ignores the relevance of Plato's criticism for all forms of writing, a point reinforced in the deliberate gaps and the related discussion of language in the *Cratylus*.
2. What do the deliberate gaps refer to if not the Theory of Principles? Do we simply dismiss these passages?
3. If we do not identify the Idea of the Good with the One, how do we account for its centrality in the *Republic*? If we regard it as ethical, do we simply dismiss the clear epistemological and metaphysical implications for the Good found in the allegories of the sun, the cave and the Divided Line?
4. If we reject the Theory of Principles, we are left with a series of disconnected Forms with no hierarchical relationship between them. Is it credible to regard this as a central theory of Plato's metaphysics? It is possible, of course, to regard the Good as central to the *Republic*, but not see it playing a major role in how we should interpret other dialogues; the Tübingen School prefers to see the Good as central to a metaphysical system underpinning Plato's entire corpus.
5. Cherniss rejects Aristotle's testimonia, claiming that it falls short on those occasions when it can be 'controlled' by the dialogues. Yet the opposite is the case, as has been demonstrated: Aristotle reflects Plato's views in the *Timaeus*, for example; even if this is not the most sympathetic interpretation that could be offered, it has not simply been falsified. The Schleiermacheans would seem to have a solid methodological basis to attack the Tübingen School for using testimonia to interpret the dialogues, rather than simply relying upon the dialogues themselves; this criticism is rendered moot by Plato's own reservations about writing.

6. If we reject the Theory of Principles, how do we account for attempts in the Old Academy to systematise Plato, which do not appear to relate very closely to the dialogues?
7. Attacks on the Tübingen School tend to focus on the notion of an 'esoteric Plato' which is a straw man set up by the Schleiermacheans themselves, not an actual Tübingen School position, or on the authenticity of the *Seventh Letter*, which is a non-issue since the presentation of the Unwritten Doctrines identified there can be located in other sources whose authenticity is beyond question.

The Tübingen School either offers responses to all of these issues or avoids the problem entirely as part of a coherent analysis. The Schleiermacheans offer an interpretation which claims to be based on what Plato says, but then dismisses his texts when it does not suit their interpretation. It is apparent which solution is the more persuasive.

Abbreviations

Adv. Math.	Sextus Empiricus, *Against the Mathematicians*
APo	Aristotle, *Posterior Analytics*
Cra.	Plato, *Cratylus*
Criti.	Plato, *Critias*
DCMS	Iamblichus, *De communi mathematica scientia*
EE	Aristotle, *Eudemian Ethics*
Enn.	Plotinus, *Enneads*
Epist. VII	Plato, *Seventh Letter*
In Parm.	Proclus, *Commentary on the Parmenides*
In Phys.	Simplicius, *On Aristotle's Physics*
Met.	Aristotle, *Metaphysics*
NE	Aristotle, *Nicomachean Ethics*
Parm.	Plato, *Parmenides*
Phd.	Plato, *Phaedo*
Phdr.	Plato, *Phaedrus*
Phlb.	Plato, *Philebus*
Plt.	Plato, *Statesman*
Prt.	Plato, *Protagoras*
Rep.	Plato, *Republic*
Soph.	Plato, *Sophist*
Symp.	Plato, *Symposium*
Theol. Plat.	Proclus, *Platonic Theology*
Tim.	Plato, *Timaeus*
TP	*Testimonia Platonica* (in Gaiser 1968: 441–557)

References

Ancient Sources

Aristoxenus. *Die harmonischen Fragmente*. Ed. by P. Marquard. Berlin: Weidmannsche Buchhandlung, 1868.

Iamblichus. *De communi mathematica scientia*. Ed. by N. Festa and U. Klein. Stuttgart: Teubner, 1975.

Plato. *Plato in Twelve Volumes*. Vols. 5 & 6. Trans. by P. Shorey. Cambridge, MA: Harvard University Press, 1969.

Philebus. Trans. with notes and commentary by J. C. B. Gosling. Oxford: Clarendon Press, 1975.

Philebus. In *Plato. Complete Works*. Ed. by J. M. Cooper and D. S. Hutchinson; trans. by D. Frede. Indianapolis, IN: Hackett, 1997, 398–456.

Simplicius. *On Aristotle Physics 1.1–2*. Trans. by S. Menn. London: Bloomsbury, 2022.

On Aristotle Physics 1.5–9. Trans. by H. Baltussen, M. Share, M. Atkinson, and I. Mueller; intro. by R. Sorabji. London: Bloomsbury, 2012.

Secondary Literature

Annas, J. (1999). *Platonic Ethics. Old and New*. Ithaca, NY: Cornell University Press.

Baltzly, D. (1996).'"To an Unhypothetical First Principle" in Plato's *Republic*'. *History of Philosophy Quarterly* 13, 149–165.

Böckh, A. [1808] (1872). 'Kritik der Übersetzung des Platon von Schleiermacher'. *Heidelbergische Jährbuch der Literatur für Philologie* I 1. Reprinted in A. Böckh, *Gesammelte Kleine Schriften Siebenter Band. Kritiken*. Leipzig: Teubner, 1–38.

Broadie, S. (2021). *Plato's Sun-Like Good. Dialectic in the* Republic. Cambridge: Cambridge University Press.

Burnyeat, M. and M. Frede (2015). *The Pseudo-Platonic* Seventh Letter. Ed. by D. Scott. Oxford: Oxford University Press.

Büsching, A. F. (1774). *Grundriß einer Geschichte der Philosophie*. Vol. 2. Berlin: Bosse.

Cherniss, H. (1936). 'The Philosophical Economy of the Theory of Ideas'. *American Journal of Philology* 57, 445–456.

(1944). *Aristotle's Criticism of Plato and the Academy*. Baltimore, MD: Johns Hopkins University Press.

(1945). *The Riddle of the Early Academy*. Berkeley, CA: University of California Press.

Corrigan, K. (2023). *A Less Familiar Plato. From* Phaedo *to* Philebus. Cambridge: Cambridge University Press.

Corrigan, K. and E. Glazov-Corrigan (2004). *Plato's Dialectic at Play. Argument, Structure and Myth in the* Symposium. University Park, PA: Pennsylvania State University Press.

D'Ancona, C. (2000). 'La doctrine des principes: Syrianus comme source textuelle et doctrinale de Proclus. 1ère Partie: Histoire du problème'. In C. Steel and A.-P. Segonds (eds.), *Proclus et la Théologie Platonicienne. Actes du Colloque International de Louvain (13–16 mai 1998). En l'honneur de H. D. Saffrey et L. G. Westerink*. Leuven: Leuven University Press, 189–225.

De Cesaris, G. (2023). 'The Chicken or the Egg? Aristotle on Speusippus' Reasons to Deny the Principle Is (the) Good'. *Apeiron* 56, 105–130.

Dillon, J. M. (2003). *The Heirs of Plato. A Study of the Old Academy (347–274 BC)*. Oxford: Clarendon Press.

Dillon, J. and L. Brisson, eds. (2010). *Plato's* Philebus. *Selected Papers from the Eight Symposium Platonicum*. Sankt Augustin: Academia Verlag.

Ferber, R. and G. Damschen (2015). 'Is the Idea of the Good beyond Being? Plato's "epekeina tes ousias" Revisited'. In D. Nails and H. Tarrant (eds.), *Second Sailing. Alternative Perspectives on Plato*. Helsinki: Societas Scientiarum Fennica.

Findlay, J. N. (1974). *Plato. The Written and Unwritten Doctrines*. London: Routledge and Kegan Paul.

Fine, G. (1993). *On Ideas. Aristotle's Criticism of Plato's Theory of Forms*. Oxford: Clarendon Press.

Frede, D. (2018). 'A Superannuated Student. Aristotle and Authority in the Academy'. In J. Bryan, R. Wardy, and J. Warren (eds.), *Authors and Authorities in Ancient Philosophy*. Cambridge: Cambridge University Press, 78–101.

Gaiser, K. (1968). *Platons Ungeschriebene Lehre und geschichtlichen Begründung in der Platonischen Schule*. 2nd ed. Stuttgart: Klett.

(1980). 'Plato's Enigmatic Lecture "On the Good"'. *Phronesis* 25, 5–37.

(2012). 'Plato's Synopsis of the Mathematical Sciences'. In Nikulin (2012b), 83–120.

Gerson, L. P. (2005). *Aristotle and Other Platonists*. Ithaca, NY: Cornell University Press.

(2013). *From Plato to Platonism*. Ithaca, NY: Cornell University Press.

(2014). 'Harold Cherniss and the Study of Plato Today'. *Journal of the History of Philosophy* 52, 397–409.

(2016). 'The "Neoplatonic" Interpretation of Plato's *Parmenides*'. *International Journal of the Platonic Tradition* 10, 65–94.

(2020). *Platonism and Naturalism. The Possibility of Philosophy*. Ithaca, NY: Cornell University Press.

(2023). *Plato's Moral Realism*. Cambridge: Cambridge University Press.

Gill, C. (2002). 'Dialectic and the Dialogue Form'. In J. Annas and C. Rowe (eds.), *New Perspectives on Plato. Modern and Ancient*. Washington, DC: Center for Hellenic Studies, 145–171.

Goldhill, S. (2002). *The Invention of Prose*. Cambridge: Cambridge University Press.

Gomperz, H. (1931). 'Platons philosophisches System'. In G. Ryle (ed.), *Proceedings of the Seventh International Congress of Philosophy*. London: H. Milford, 426–431. Reprinted in Wippern (1972), 159–165.

Hackforth, R., ed. (1952). *Plato's* Phaedrus. Trans. with an introduction and commentary. Cambridge: Cambridge University Press.

Halfwassen J. (1992). *Der Aufstieg zum Einen. Untersuchungen zu Platon und Plotin*. Stuttgart: Teubner.

(2001). 'Der Ursprung der Geistmetaphysik. Die wiederentdeckte Einheit des antiken Platonismus'. In T. A. Szlezák (ed. with assistance from K. H. Stanzel), *Platonisches Philosophieren. Zehn Vorträge zu Ehren von Hans-Joachim Krämer*. Hildesheim: Olms, 47–65.

(2006). 'Proklos über die Transzendenz des Einen bei Platon'. In M. Perkams and R. Piccione (eds.), *Proklos Methode, Seelenlehre, Metaphysik*. Leiden: Brill, 363–383.

(2012). 'Monism and Dualism in Plato's Doctrine of Principles'. In Nikulin (2012b), 143–159.

(2015). *Auf den Spuren des Einen. Studien zur Metaphysik und ihrer Geschichte*. Tubingen: Mohr Siebeck.

(2021). *Plotinus, Neoplatonism and the Transcendence of the One*. Ed., trans., and intro. by C. S. O'Brien. Steubenville, OH: Franciscan University Press.

Hegel, G. W. F. [1832] (1986). *Vorlesung über die Philosophie der Religion I*. In E. Moldenhauer and K. M. Michel (eds.), *Werke in zwanzig Bänden. Theorie-Werkausgabe*. New ed., vol. 16. Frankfurt: Suhrkamp.

Hösle, V. (2019). 'The Tübingen School'. In A. Kim (ed.), *Brill's Companion to German Platonism*. Leiden: Brill, 328–348.

Ionescu, C. (2019). *On the Good Life. Thinking through the Intermediaries in Plato's* Philebus. Albany, NY: State University of New York Press.

Krämer, H. J. (1959). *Arete bei Platon und Aristoteles. Zum Wesen und zur Geschichte der Platonischen Ontologie*. Heidelberg: Universitätsverlag Winter.

(1964a). *Der Ursprung der Geistmetaphysik. Untersuchungen zur Geschichte des Platonismus zwischen Platon und Plotin*. Amsterdam: Schippers.

(1964b). 'Retraktationen zum Problem des esoterischen Platon'. *Museum Helveticum* 21, 137–167.

(1986). 'Mutamento di Paradigma nelle Richerche su Platone. Riflessioni intorno al Nuovo Libro di Giovanni Reale'. *Rivista di filosofia neoscholastica* 78, 341–352.

(1990). *Plato and the Foundations of Metaphysics. A Work on the Theory of the Principles and Unwritten Doctrines of Plato with a Collection of the Fundamental Documents*. Ed. and trans. by J. R. Catan. Albany, NY: State University of New York Press.

(2012a). '*Epekeina tēs ousias*: On Plato, *Republic* 509b'. In Nikulin (2012b), 39–64.

(2012b). 'Plato's Unwritten Doctrine'. In Nikulin (2012b), 65–81.

Kullmann, W. (1991). 'Platons Schriftkritik'. *Hermes* 119, 2–21.

Luna, C. (2000). 'La doctrine des principes: Syrianus comme source textuelle et doctrinale de Proclus. IIème partie: Analyse des textes'. In C. Steel and A.-P. Segonds (2000), *Proclus et la Théologie Platonicienne. Actes du Colloque International de Louvain (13–16 mai 1998). En l'honneur de H. D. Saffrey et L. G. Westerink*. Leuven: Leuven University Press, 227–278.

Mackenzie, M. M. (1982). 'Paradox in Plato's *Phaedrus*'. *Proceedings of the Cambridge Philological Society* n.s. 28, 64–76.

Menn, S. (2022). *Simplicius. On Aristotle Physics 1–8. General Introduction to the 12 Volumes of Translations*. London: Bloomsbury.

Migliori, M. (2020). *Lifelong Studies in Love with Plato*. Baden-Baden: Academia Verlag.

(2023). *How Plato Writes. The Educational and Protreptic Intent of the Great Student of Socrates*. Baden-Baden: Academia Verlag.

Nikulin, D. (2012a). 'Plato: Testimonia et Fragmenta'. In Nikulin (2012b), 1–38.

(2012b). *The Other Plato. The Tübingen Interpretation of Plato's Inner-Academic Teachings*. Albany, NY: State University of New York Press.

(2019). *Neoplatonism in Late Antiquity*. Oxford: Oxford University Press.

O'Brien, C. S. (2015). *The Demiurge in Ancient Thought. Secondary Gods and Divine Mediators*. Cambridge: Cambridge University Press.

(2019). 'Plato on the Absolute'. In E. Plevrakis and M. Rohstock (eds.), *Grundlegung des Absoluten? Paradigmen aus der Geschichte der Metaphysik*, Heidelberg: Universitätsverlag Winter, 15–36.

(2021a). 'Jens Halfwassen and the German Intellectual Tradition'. In Halfwassen (2021), xv–xxvii.

(2021b). 'Platonic Dialogues and Platonic Principles'. *International Journal of the Platonic Tradition* 15.1, 90–98.

(forthcoming). 'The Theory of Principles and Neoplatonic Readings of the Atlantis Myth'. In C. S. O'Brien and S. K. Wear (eds.), *Platonic Principles. Essays in Honor of Lloyd Gerson*. Steubenville, OH: Franciscan University Press.

O'Brien, C. S. and S. K. Wear (2017). 'The Figure of the Diadochos from Socrates to the Late Antique Athenian School of Neoplatonism'. In J. Finamore and S. Klitenic Wear (eds.), *Defining Platonism. Essays in Honor of the 75th Birthday of John M. Dillon*. Steubenville, OH: Franciscan University Press, 253–270.

Osborne, C. (1998). 'Was Verse the Default Form for Presocratic Philosophy?'. In C. Atherton, (ed.), *Form and Content in Didactic Poetry*. Bari: Levante Editori, 23–35.

Ostenfeld, E. M. (2010). 'The Psychology of the *Philebus*'. In Dillon and Brisson (2010), 307–312.

Owen, G. E. L. (1953). 'The Place of the *Timaeus* in Plato's Dialogues'. *Classical Quarterly* n. s. 3, 73–95.

Papandreou, M. (2024). *Aristotle's Ontology of Artefacts*. Cambridge: Cambridge University Press.

Penner, T. (2007a). 'What Is the Form of the Good the Form of? A Question about the Plot of the *Republic*?'. In D. Cairns, F. G. Herrmann, and T. Penner (eds.), *Pursuing the Good. Ethics and Metaphysics in Plato's Republic*. Edinburgh: Edinburgh University Press, 15–41.

(2007b). 'The Good, Advantage, Happiness and the Form of the Good. How Continuous with Socratic Ethics Is Platonic Ethics?'. In Cairns, Herrmann, and Penner (2007), 93–123.

Politis, V. (2020). 'Plato's *Seventh Letter*. A Close and Dispassionate Reading of the Philosophical Section'. *Classics Ireland* 27, 56–77.

Reale, G. (1990). 'Introduction. The "Italian Plato" of Hans Krämer'. In Krämer (1990), xvii–xxvi.

(1997). *Toward a New Interpretation of Plato*. Washington, DC: Catholic University of America Press.

(2010). *Per una nuova interpretazione di Platone alla luce della 'dottrine non scritte'*. Milan: Bompiani.

Reale, G. and D. Antiseri (2010). *Historia de la filosofía I. De la Antigüedad a la Edad Media. Filosofía antigua-pagana*. Barcelona: Herder.

Rist, J. M. (1962). 'The Neoplatonic One and Plato's *Parmenides*'. *Transactions of the American Philological Association* 93, 389–401.

Robin, L. (1908). *Le théorie platonicienne des Idées et des Nombres d'après Aristote. Étude historique et critique*. Paris: Alcan.

Rowe, C. J. (1986). 'The argument and structure of Plato's *Phaedrus*'. *Proceedings of the Cambridge Philological Society* n.s. 32, 106–125.

(2007). 'The Form of the Good and the Good in Plato's *Republic*'. In Cairns, Herrmann and Penner (eds.), *Pursuing the Good. Ethics and Metaphysics in Plato's* Republic. Edinburgh: Edinburgh University Press, 124–153.

(2014). 'Methodologies for Reading Plato'. In Oxford Handbooks Editorial Board, *The Oxford Handbook of Topics in Philosophy*. Oxford: Oxford University Press. https://doi.org/10.1093/oxfordhb/9780199935314.013.28.

Sayre, K. M. (2005). *Plato's Late Ontology. A Riddle Resolved*. Las Vegas, NV: Parmenides.

Schleiermacher, F. (1804). *Platons Werke von F. Schleiermacher, Volume I 1*. Berlin: Reimer.

Sedley, D. (2008). *Creationism and Its Critics in Antiquity*. Berkeley, CA: University of California Press.

(2016). 'An Introduction to Plato's Theory of Forms'. *Royal Institute of Philosophy Supplement* 78, 3–22.

(2021). 'Xenocrates' Invention of Platonism'. In M. Erler, J. E. Heßler, and F. M. Petrucci (eds.), *Authority and Authoritative Texts in the Platonist Tradition*. Cambridge: Cambridge University Press, 12–37.

Seel, G. (2007). 'Is Plato's Conception of the Form of the Good Contradictory?'. In D. Cairns, F. G. Herrmann, and T. Penner (eds.), *Pursuing the Good. Ethics and Metaphysics in Plato's* Republic. Edinburgh: Edinburgh University Press, 168–196.

Shorey, P. (1903). *The Unity of Plato's Thought*. Chicago, IL: University of Chicago Press.

Smith, C. C. (2023). 'The Senses of Apeiron in *Philebus* 16b–27c'. *Méthexis* 25, 167–184.

Sorabji, R. (2012). 'Introduction'. In *Simplicius. On Aristotle Physics 1.5–9*. London: Bloomsbury, 1–12.

Steel, C. (2002). 'A Neoplatonic Speusippus'. In M. Barbanti, G. R. Giardina, and P. Manganaro (eds.), *Hénosis Kaì Philía, Unione e Amicizia. Omaggio a Francesco Romano*. Catania: Cooperativa universitaria editrice catanese di magistero, 469–476.

Strauss, L. (2000). *On Tyranny. Including the Strauss–Kojève Correspondence.* V. Gourevitch and M. S. Roth (eds.). Chicago, IL: University of Chicago Press.

Sung-hyun Yang, D. (2024). 'Aristotle's Critique of Form-Number'. *Elenchos* 45, 229–254.

Szlezák, T. A. (1985). *Platon und die Schriftlichkeit der Philosophie. Interpretationen zu den frühen und mittleren Dialogen.* Berlin: De Gruyter.

(1999). *Reading Plato.* London: Routledge.

(2004). *Das Bild des Dialektikers in Platons späten Dialogen. Platon und die Schriftlichkeit der Philosophie Teil II.* Berlin: De Gruyter.

(2012a). 'The Idea of the Good as *Archē* in Plato's *Republic*'. In Nikulin (2012b), 121–142.

(2012b). 'The Tübingen Approach'. In G. A. Press (ed.), *The Continuum Companion to Plato.* London: Bloomsbury, 303–305.

(2019a). *Aufsätze zur griechischen Literatur und Philosophie.* Baden-Baden: Academia Verlag.

(2019b). 'Friedrich Schleiermachers's Theory of the Platonic Dialogue and Its Legacy'. In A. Kim (ed.), *Brill's Companion to German Platonism.* Leiden: Brill, 165–191.

(2021). *Platon. Meisterdenker der Antike.* Munich: Beck.

Taylor, C. C. W. (2002). 'The Origins of Our Present Paradigms'. In J. Annas and C. Rowe (eds.), *New Perspectives on Plato. Modern and Ancient.* Washington, DC: Center for Hellenic Studies, 73–84.

Trendelenburg, F. A. (1826). *Platonis de ideis et numeris doctrina ex Aristotele illustrata.* Leipzig: Vogel.

Vlastos, G. (1963). 'Review of *Arete bei Platon und Aristoteles* by H. J. Krämer'. *Gnomon* 41, 641–655. Reprinted as 'On Plato's Oral Doctrine'. In Vlastos (1973), 379–398.

(1973). *Platonic Studies.* Princeton, NJ: Princeton University Press.

Wilamovitz-Moellendorff, U. von (1919). *Platon.* 2 vols. Berlin: Wiedmannsche Verlagsbuchhandlung.

Wippern, J. ed. (1972). *Das Problem der Ungeschriebene Lehre Platons.* Darmstadt: Wissenschaftliche Buchgesellschaft.

Acknowledgements

I am extremely grateful to Prof. James Warren, both for offering this Element a home in the Cambridge Elements in Ancient Philosophy series and for guiding it along the various stages of its journey, as well as for his comments on the manuscript. The Element has been greatly improved by the feedback of Prof. John Dillon and the anonymous reviewers of the Press; equally I have benefitted from discussions on this topic with Profs. Lloyd Gerson, Sarah Klitenic Wear, István Czachesz, and Kevin Corrigan. Additionally, I am grateful to Fr Leonard Moloney SJ and Prof. Dominic O'Meara. A special word of thanks to everyone at the Press and at Integra for making this Element possible, especially Priyanka Durai, the production manager; Shalini Priyatharshini, the project management executive; Ami Naramor, the copy editor; and Adam Hooper, the Cambridge Elements senior content manager.

My interest in Plato's Unwritten Doctrines was stimulated by the period I spent at the University of Heidelberg with Prof. Jens Halfwassen as an Alexander von Humboldt Fellow and as a Fritz Thyssen Fellow. The Dominican Studium Generale in Dublin provided me with an intellectual home where I was able to write this Element; I am extremely grateful to the Dominican community of St Saviour's Priory for all of their support, especially Fr Terence Crotty OP. Heartfelt gratitude also goes to my father, Raymond O'Brien, and sister, Dr Zeldine O'Brien.

Cambridge Elements

Ancient Philosophy

James Warren
University of Cambridge

James Warren is Professor of Ancient Philosophy at the University of Cambridge. He is the author of *Epicurus and Democritean Ethics* (Cambridge, 2002), *Facing Death: Epicurus and his Critics* (2004), *Presocratics* (2007) and *The Pleasures of Reason in Plato, Aristotle and the Hellenistic Hedonists* (Cambridge, 2014). He is also the editor of *The Cambridge Companion to Epicurus* (Cambridge, 2009), and joint editor of *Authors and Authorities in Ancient Philosophy* (Cambridge, 2018).

About the Series

The Elements in Ancient Philosophy series deals with a wide variety of topics and texts in ancient Greek and Roman philosophy, written by leading scholars in the field. Taking a theme, question, or type of argument, some Elements explore it across antiquity and beyond. Others look in detail at an ancient author, a specific work, or a part of a longer work, considering its structure, content, and significance, or explore more directly ancient perspectives on modern philosophical questions.

Cambridge Elements

Ancient Philosophy

Elements in the Series

Relative Change
Matthew Duncombe

Plato's Ion: *Poetry, Expertise, and Inspiration*
Franco V. Trivigno

Aristotle on Ontological Priority in the Categories
Ana Laura Edelhoff

The Method of Hypothesis and the Nature of Soul in Plato's Phaedo
John Palmer

Aristotle on Women: Physiology, Psychology, and Politics
Sophia M. Connell

The Hedonism of Eudoxus of Cnidus
Richard Davies

Properties in Ancient Metaphysics
Anna Marmodoro

Vice in Ancient Philosophy: Plato and Aristotle on Moral Ignorance and Corruption of Character
Karen Margrethe Nielsen

Stoic Eros
Simon Shogry

Suspension of Belief
Daniel Vázquez

Contemplation and Civic Happiness in Plato and Aristotle
Dominic Scott

Plato's Unwritten Doctrines
Carl Séan O'Brien

A full series listing is available at: www.cambridge.org/EIAP

www.ingramcontent.com/pod-product-compliance
Lightning Source LLC
LaVergne TN
LVHW011859060526
838200LV00054B/4430